From Coronado to Escalante:

The Explorers of the Spanish Southwest

General Editor

William H. Goetzmann
Jack S. Blanton, Sr., Chair in History
  University of Texas at Austin

Consulting Editor

Tom D. Crouch
Chairman, Department of Aeronautics
  National Air and Space Museum
  Smithsonian Institution

WORLD EXPLORERS

From Coronado to Escalante:
The Explorers of the Spanish Southwest

John Miller Morris

CHELSEA HOUSE PUBLISHERS

New York · Philadelphia

On the cover   Map of New Mexico by Bernardo de Miera y
Pacheco; Wyeth's portrait of Coronado

Chelsea House Publishers
Editor-in-Chief   Remmel Nunn
Managing Editor   Karyn Gullen Browne
Copy Chief   Mark Rifkin
Picture Editor   Adrian G. Allen
Art Director   Maria Epes
Assistant Art Director   Howard Brotman
Series Design   Loraine Machlin
Manufacturing Director   Gerald Levine
Systems Manager   Lindsey Ottman
Production Manager   Joseph Romano
Production Coordinator   Marie Claire Cebrián

World Explorers
Senior Editor   Sean Dolan

Staff for FROM CORONADO TO ESCALANTE: THE EXPLORERS OF THE
SPANISH SOUTHWEST
Senior Copy Editor   Laurie Kahn
Picture Researcher   Nisa Rauschenberg
Senior Designer   Basia Niemczyc

7 9 8 6

Library of Congress Cataloging-in-Publication Data

Morris, John Miller
   From Coronado to Escalante: the explorers of the Spanish
Southwest/John Miller Morris.
      p.   cm.—(World explorers)
. Includes bibliographical references and index.
   Summary: Traces the history of Spanish exploration of the
American Southwest and Mexico.
   ISBN 0-7910-1300-6
        0-7910-1523-8 (pbk)
   1. Southwest, New—Discovery and exploration—Spanish—
Juvenile literature.   2. Mexico—Discovery and exploration—
Spanish—Juvenile literature.   3. Explorers—Southwest, New—
History—Juvenile literature.   4. Explorers—Mexico—History—
Juvenile literature.   5. Explorers—Spain—History—Juvenile
literature.   [1. Southwest, New—Discovery and exploration—
Spanish.   2. Mexico—Discovery and exploration—Spanish.
3. Explorers.]   I. Title.   II. Series.
                                                    91-34046
F799.M85   1992   CIP
979'.01—dc20   AC

CONTENTS

WORLD EXPLORERS

THE EARLY EXPLORERS

Herodotus and the Explorers of the Classical Age
Marco Polo and the Medieval Explorers
The Viking Explorers

THE FIRST GREAT AGE OF DISCOVERY

Jacques Cartier, Samuel de Champlain, and the Explorers of Canada
Christopher Columbus and the First Voyages to the New World
From Coronado to Escalante: The Explorers of the Spanish Southwest
Hernando de Soto and the Explorers of the American South
Sir Francis Drake and the Struggle for an Ocean Empire
Vasco da Gama and the Portuguese Explorers
La Salle and the Explorers of the Mississippi
Ferdinand Magellan and the Discovery of the World Ocean
Pizarro, Orellana, and the Exploration of the Amazon
The Search for the Northwest Passage
Giovanni da Verrazano and the Explorers of the Atlantic Coast

THE SECOND GREAT AGE OF DISCOVERY

Roald Amundsen and the Quest for the South Pole
Daniel Boone and the Opening of the Ohio Country
Captain James Cook and the Explorers of the Pacific
The Explorers of Alaska
John Charles Frémont and the Great Western Reconnaissance
Alexander von Humboldt, Colossus of Exploration
Lewis and Clark and the Route to the Pacific
Alexander Mackenzie and the Explorers of Canada
Robert Peary and the Quest for the North Pole
Zebulon Pike and the Explorers of the American Southwest
John Wesley Powell and the Great Surveys of the American West
Jedediah Smith and the Mountain Men of the American West
Henry Stanley and the European Explorers of Africa
Lt. Charles Wilkes and the Great U.S. Exploring Expedition

THE THIRD GREAT AGE OF DISCOVERY

Apollo to the Moon
The Explorers of the Undersea World
The First Men in Space
The Mission to Mars and Beyond
Probing Deep Space

CHELSEA HOUSE PUBLISHERS

Into the Unknown

Michael Collins

It is difficult to define most eras in history with any precision, but not so the space age. On October 4, 1957, it burst on us with little warning when the Soviet Union launched *Sputnik*, a 184-pound cannonball that circled the globe once every 96 minutes. Less than 4 years later, the Soviets followed this first primitive satellite with the flight of Yury Gagarin, a 27-year-old fighter pilot who became the first human to orbit the earth. The Soviet Union's success prompted President John F. Kennedy to decide that the United States should "land a man on the moon and return him safely to earth" before the end of the 1960s. We now had not only a space age but a space race.

I was born in 1930, exactly the right time to allow me to participate in Project Apollo, as the U.S. lunar program came to be known. As a young man growing up, I often found myself too young to do the things I wanted—or suddenly too old, as if someone had turned a switch at midnight. But for Apollo, 1930 was the perfect year to be born, and I was very lucky. In 1966 I enjoyed circling the earth for three days, and in 1969 I flew to the moon and laughed at the sight of the tiny earth, which I could cover with my thumbnail.

How the early explorers would have loved the view from space! With one glance Christopher Columbus could have plotted his course and reassured his crew that the world was indeed round. In 90 minutes Magellan could have looked down at every port of call in the *Victoria's* three-year circumnavigation of the globe. Given a chance to map their route from orbit, Lewis and Clark could have told President Jefferson that there was no easy Northwest Passage but that a continent of exquisite diversity awaited their scrutiny.

In a physical sense, we have already gone to most places that we can. That is not to say that there are not new adventures awaiting us deep in the sea or on the red plains of Mars, but more important than reaching new places will be understanding those we have already visited. There are vital gaps in our understanding of how our planet works as an ecosystem and how our planet fits into the infinite order of the universe. The next great age may well be the age of assimilation, in which we use microscope and telescope to evaluate what we have discovered and put that knowledge to use. The adventure of being first to reach may be replaced by the satisfaction of being first to grasp. Surely that is a form of exploration as vital to our well-being, and perhaps even survival, as the distinction of being the first to explore a specific geographical area.

The explorers whose stories are told in the books of this series did not just sail perilous seas, scale rugged mountains, traverse blistering deserts, dive to the depths of the ocean, or land on the moon. Their voyages and expeditions were journeys of mind as much as of time and distance, through which they—and all of mankind—were able to reach a greater understanding of our universe. That challenge remains, for all of us. The imperative is to see, to understand, to develop knowledge that others can use, to help nurture this planet that sustains us all. Perhaps being born in 1975 will be as lucky for a new generation of explorer as being born in 1930 was for Neil Armstrong, Buzz Aldrin, and Mike Collins.

The Reader's Journey

William H. Goetzmann

This volume is one of a series that takes us with the great
explorers of the ages on bold journeys over the oceans and
the continents and into outer space. As we travel along
with these imaginative and courageous journeyers, we
share their adventures and their knowledge. We also get
a glimpse of that mysterious and inextinguishable fire that
burned in the breast of men such as Magellan and Columbus—the fire that has propelled all those throughout
the ages who have been driven to leave behind family and
friends for a voyage into the unknown.

No one has ever satisfactorily explained the urge to explore, the drive to go to the "back of beyond." It is certain
that it has been present in man almost since he began
walking erect and first ventured across the African savan-
nas. Sparks from that same fire fueled the transoceanic
explorers of the Ice Age, who led their people across the
vast plain that formed a land bridge between Asia and
North America, and the astronauts and scientists who de-
termined that man must reach the moon.

Besides an element of adventure, all exploration in-
volves an element of mystery. We must not confuse exploration with discovery. Exploration is a purposeful
human activity—a search for something. Discovery may
be the end result of that search; it may also be an accident,

as when Columbus found a whole new world while searching for the Indies. Often, the explorer may not even realize the full significance of what he has discovered, as was the case with Columbus. Exploration, on the other hand, is the product of a cultural or individual curiosity; it is a unique process that has enabled mankind to know and understand the world's oceans, continents, and polar regions. It is at the heart of scientific thinking. One of its most significant aspects is that it teaches people to ask the right questions; by doing so, it forces us to reevaluate what we think we know and understand. Thus knowledge progresses, and we are driven constantly to a new awareness and appreciation of the universe in all its infinite variety.

The motivation for exploration is not always pure. In his fascination with the new, man often forgets that others have been there before him. For example, the popular notion of the discovery of America overlooks the complex Indian civilizations that had existed there for thousands of years before the arrival of Europeans. Man's desire for conquest, riches, and fame is often linked inextricably with his quest for the unknown, but a story that touches so closely on the human essence must of necessity treat war as well as peace, avarice with generosity, both pride and humility, frailty and greatness. The story of exploration is above all a story of humanity and of man's understanding of his place in the universe.

The WORLD EXPLORERS series has been divided into four sections. The first treats the explorers of the ancient world, the Viking explorers of the 9th through the 11th centuries, and Marco Polo and the medieval explorers. The rest of the series is divided into three great ages of exploration. The first is the era of Columbus and Magellan: the period spanning the 15th and 16th centuries, which saw the discovery and exploration of the New World and the world ocean. The second might be called the age of science and imperialism, the era made possible by the scientific advances of the 17th century, which witnessed the discovery of the world's last two undiscovered continents, Australia and Antarctica, the mapping of all the continents and oceans, and the establishment of colonies all over the world. The third great age refers to the most ambitious quests of the 20th century—the probing of space and of the ocean's depths.

As we reach out into the darkness of outer space and other galaxies, we come to better understand how our ancestors confronted *oecumene,* or the vast earthly unknown. We learn once again the meaning of an unknown 18th-century sea captain's advice to navigators:

> And if by chance you make a landfall on the shores of another sea in a far country inhabited by savages and barbarians, remember you this: the greatest danger and the surest hope lies not with fires and arrows but in the quicksilver hearts of men.

At its core, exploration is a series of moral dramas. But it is these dramas, involving new lands, new people, and exotic ecosystems of staggering beauty, that make the explorers' stories not only moral tales but also some of the greatest adventure stories ever recorded. They represent the process of learning in its most expansive and vivid forms. We see that real life, past and present, transcends even the adventures of the starship *Enterprise.*

Entradas

In the early spring of 1539, a strange procession wound its way through the remote Indian villages strewn among the valleys of Mexico's magnificent Sierra Madre Occidental. Indian messengers bearing a sacred gourd rattle decorated with strings of tiny bells and two feathers, one red and one white, would arrive in the villages first to announce the approach of the travelers and to inform the villagers that a shaman, or medicine man, was among them. Soon after, a friendly group of about 40 newcomers, most of them Indians, would enter the village. They would stop to rest, eat, and socialize. Some would inquire about the rough trails ahead. As the curious, dark-eyed Indian children and adults turned out to see the visitors, two men in particular attracted strong stares. To the bronzed Indians of northwest Mexico, the two men were strange indeed, for one was black as night, and one was white as day.

The mystic rattle belonged to the black man, by far the more sensational looking of the two. He was dressed colorfully, adorned with turquoises and bright feathers, and the bells he wore on his arms and ankles jingled with his every movement and gesture. The Indian women especially found him attractive, and soon they were gathered about him. Who was this tall, muscular, dark-skinned shaman? the Indians wondered. He was known to his companions as Black Stephen, Stephen the Moor, or simply the Moor, but his true name was Esteban de Dorantes. His pale friend, Fray Marcos de Niza, was a French priest of the Catholic Franciscan order. Both of these men had

From 1492 to 1542, Spanish navigators and conquistadores surged across half the globe. During those years, the Spanish empire acquired more territory than the Romans had taken in five centuries of conquest, and Spanish armor was on the march in the New World from the southern tip of South America to Oregon.

A 16th-century European map of the New World. By 1540, despite the Europeans' inaccurate geographic conception of the two continents, Spanish entradas (expeditions to the interior) had penetrated to the heart of South America and Mexico. But the greater Southwest of the present-day United States was still untouched by a major Spanish incursion, and it remained a land of mystery.

been blown into the North American interior on the winds of the Spanish conquest.

Those winds had been raging with hurricane force for the previous half century. The Spanish adventurers who followed Christopher Columbus to the New World and laid claim to it in the name of God and king were called conquistadores, and in their relentless quest for gold, glory, and new territory for the Spanish crown they imposed themselves on the lands and native peoples of the Americas with furious determination and ruthlessness. Their caravels appeared off the Atlantic coasts of the New World in the early years of the 16th century, and soon the first *entradas*—expeditions to the interior—were under way.

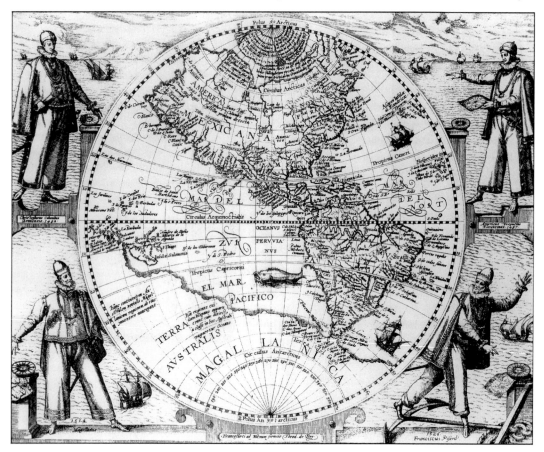

The entradas of the conquistadores were part military incursion and part expedition of discovery. For the native civilizations of the New World, such as the Inca and Aztec empires, they were a military and cultural Armageddon. The most famous (or infamous) of the entradas were those of the conquistadores Hernán Cortés and Francisco Pizarro. In 1519, Cortés marched an army of 500 Spanish troops into Mexico and, using terror, guile, and sheer force of arms, destroyed the powerful Aztec empire, acquiring great wealth and renown for himself in the process. Cortés became one of the most powerful men in the New World, and Mexico became New Spain. In 1532, Pizarro accomplished a similar feat, leading a tiny Spanish force into

The legend of El Dorado ("the golden man"), a New World city of riches ruled by a golden king, drew many adventurous Spaniards to North and South America. The legend was inspired by the Muysca Indians of Peru, who, as shown here in this 16th-century illustration, honored a new chieftain by annointing his body with balsam and then blowing gold dust on him, thus creating a kind of golden man.

In 1528, the entrada of conquistador Pánfilo de Narváez disintegrated along the Gulf of Mexico. Alligators, disease, starvation, and Indians claimed all but four members of the expedition. The survivors, led by the Spaniard Álvar Núñez Cabeza de Vaca, walked back to Mexico—it took them eight years to get home—thus becoming the first non-Indians to see the inland Southwest.

the Peruvian Andes. Pizarro and his fierce conquistadores routed the massive armies of the Inca empire, subjugated its peoples, and plundered its riches, which included untold tons of gold artifacts.

Not all of the entradas of the conquistadores met with conquest and glory, however. Many of them were episodes of folly and disaster for the Spaniards. In 1541, for example, Gonzalo Pizarro, the savage brother of Francisco, led an entrada into the Amazon rainforest in search of the mythical golden city of El Dorado. The expedition degenerated into a nightmare of starvation, cannibalism, and death, and Pizarro was lucky to emerge alive from the Peruvian jungles 16 months later. Others were not so lucky. In 1528, a grandiose conquistador named Pánfilo de Narváez, at the head of an expedition numbering 400, landed on the Florida coast near Tampa Bay and pushed inland.

The invaders, encumbered by their heavy European armor, soon found themselves hopelessly mired in the Florida swamplands and besieged by mosquitoes, hostile Indians, and numerous alligators and snakes. They retreated to the beach only to find that their ships were gone. Building makeshift boats from the local timber, they attempted to sail along the coast of the Gulf of Mexico to the Spanish colonies in Mexico. Storms, starvation, disease, and Indians decimated the party. Narváez deserted them and was never seen or heard from again. In fact, only four members of the original expeditionary force were heard from again, but not until eight years later. One of the survivors was a black man, Esteban de Dorantes, the Moor. Esteban was the slave of another of the four, conquistador Andrés Dorantes. The third was Alonso de Castillo. The one destined to be most well known to history was a nobleman named Álvar Núñez Cabeza de Vaca.

When these weary, bedraggled, and bearded wanderers appeared near Culiacán on the west coast of Mexico in 1536, claiming to be survivors of the lost Florida expedition of Pánfilo de Narváez, they were immediately brought to the viceroy of New Spain, Don Antonio de Mendoza. Cabeza de Vaca and Esteban then told the viceroy a remarkable story of adventure and survival.

When the flimsy makeshift boats of the beleaguered Narváez expedition disintegrated along the Gulf of Mexico following their retreat from Florida, Cabeza de Vaca, Esteban, Dorantes, and Castillo found themselves marooned on the Texas coast near present-day Galveston. After a period of enslavement by coastal Indians, they escaped and made their way west, surviving by befriending the various nomadic Indian tribes of Texas and Mexico. Traveling and living with the Indians, they wandered across southern Texas, moving gradually westward through lands as yet unseen by non-Indian eyes. As the years went by and their odyssey continued, the Moor and the Spaniard learned the ways of the Indians and, more important, they grew to respect them. Esteban, no longer a slave among white Europeans but a free man traveling across the vast, open landscapes of the American Southwest, proved adept at assimilating the cultural traditions of the Native Americans. He assumed the trappings of a shaman, and both he and Cabeza de Vaca acquired a reputation as healers, which further helped to smooth their passage among the

A Hopi kachina doll representing a black man recalls the passage of Esteban through the Arizona pueblos. Esteban was the first black man the Hopis had ever encountered, and he acquired a legendary status that persisted among the Indians long after he was gone.

various tribes. Finally, after eight long years, Cabeza de Vaca and Esteban found themselves among Christians once again.

The viceroy listened to their tale with growing astonishment, for it was an amazing story indeed. After his conquest of the Aztecs, Cortés had sent entradas and smaller expeditions to various parts of Mexico and Central America, but the lands to New Spain's north—the Southwest of the present-day United States, including New Mexico, Arizona, and Texas—remained unknown. Here was the first concrete intelligence the Spanish were to receive about the lands and inhabitants of the interior of the American Southwest. Cabeza de Vaca, Esteban, and their two companions had seen things no other Europeans had seen. Apparently, the continent was larger than anyone had imagined. They described great expanses of prairie and desert, high plateaus and rugged cordilleras, great rivers and escarpments, and large, horned, shaggy beasts that lived on the plains and resembled cattle. But the part of their story that most interested the viceroy concerned rumors the two travelers had heard among the Indians: rumors about a land rich in gold and turquoises located somewhere to the north of the route they had taken to Mexico. The Spanish would soon connect these rumors to legends of their own about seven golden cities and give them the Indian name for the region—the Seven Cities of Cíbola.

Mendoza, no doubt thinking about the riches found by Cortés and Pizarro in Mexico and South America, began to make plans for an entrada. But first, he would send a small reconnaissance party to gather more information. Cabeza de Vaca had departed for Spain—this remarkable Spaniard would continue his career as an explorer and Indian-rights advocate in South America—so Mendoza recruited an intrepid Franciscan missionary, Fray Marcos de Niza, to lead the party. Esteban, the former slave, would act as guide.

And so the two holy men, now agents of the viceroy and the Spanish crown, one dressed in Indian finery and the other wearing a simple Franciscan habit of gray cloth, passed through the cordilleran villages in March 1539. They asked pointed questions about the lands to the north and listened excitedly to talk of the great cities of Cíbola and the gold and precious stones to be found there. Occasionally Esteban would pray over a sick Indian, his bells tinkling sweetly as he performed the ritual gestures of healing. But within a year, the cheerful sound of Esteban's bells would be replaced by the heavy clanging of Spanish armor as the entrada of Francisco Vázquez de Coronado passed on its way northward.

Like many Spanish conquistadores, Don Francisco Vázquez de Coronado, governor of the province of New Galicia in Mexico, was drawn to the New World by the promise of riches and glory to be won there. Coronado would get his chance to win both; he was the man chosen to lead a massive entrada into the interior of the American Southwest in search of the fabled Seven Cities of Cíbola.

The Turquoise Trail

Although they walked every step of the way, Esteban and the friar made fair progress after their early March departure from Culiacán, the northernmost Spanish frontier settlement in Mexico. Crossing a series of swift, mountain-flank tributaries that flowed westward to the Pacific Ocean, they soon reached the Rio Fuerte. On March 23, 1539, they arrived at a native village called Vacapa, and there they parted company—forever. Fray Marcos sent Esteban ahead with instructions to search for "some inhabited and rich country"—namely Cíbola—and to send messengers back to Vacapa once he had found such a place. Esteban was illiterate, so they would use a code. He was to build wooden crosses and send them back to Fray Marcos. The bigger the cross, the greater the city and its treasures.

Esteban pushed northward while Fray Marcos remained at Vacapa gathering information on the geography of the nearby Pacific Coast area. Four days after the departure of Esteban, several excited Indian couriers arrived at Vacapa bearing a cross the size of a man. This was stupendous news, for the friar had instructed Esteban to send a cross "a span [nine inches] in size" if he discovered a "moderate" city and two spans if he found something a bit more interesting. He was to send back a large cross only if he came upon something comparable to the old Aztec capital of Tenochtitlán, a huge and fabulously wealthy city that had stood, before Cortés's conquest, on the site of Mexico City.

A 1528 map of Mexico City, the seat of the Spanish colonial empire of New Spain. When Fray Marcos de Niza returned to the city in July 1539, claiming he had seen Cíbola and its riches, word quickly spread, and Viceroy Mendoza lost no time in planning an entrada.

This man-sized cross would signify a great discovery. And there was more—one of the Indians carrying the huge cross claimed to have seen the marvels of this rich kingdom in the north. It was called Cíbola, and it lay 30 days north of Esteban's whereabouts. In Cíbola, the Indian assured the priest, were seven towering, multistoried cities where precious turquoises were so common they were used for the decoration of doors!

Fray Marcos set off after Esteban, following his footsteps along one of the most ancient trading routes in the New World—the turquoise trail. For centuries the native peoples of the greater southwest region had used the trail to transport and barter commodities, including turquoises, pretty seashells from the Gulf of California, colorful mineral pigments, buffalo robes from the interior, and exotic feathers. As the Franciscan trudged along this ancient pathway between the ocean and the distant mesa lands of the interior, his excitement grew, for many of the Indians he encountered and questioned knew of Cíbola; some claimed to have been there. And Esteban continued to build huge crosses and to send back couriers to show the way.

But the messengers also brought disturbing news about Esteban himself. He was reportedly traveling with a large retinue of followers, including a personal guard of Indian warriors and what could be described only as a harem of admiring young Indian women. Like a great holy man on a pilgrimage he passed from village to village, accepting gifts, accumulating turquoises, distributing blessings, and collecting new followers along the way. Fray Marcos was troubled by this news. It sounded as if Esteban was going a little too far with his medicine man act. Troubled, the friar picked up his pace and hurried along the trail.

By now, Esteban was following the turquoise trail across the first of two *despoblados*—desolate, cactus-strewn wastelands—he would encounter on his way to Cíbola. Extra water and experienced local guides proved essential in crossing this unforgiving region of thorns, heat, and thirst, known today as the Sonoran Desert and called by the Indians the Land of Everlasting Summer. After a four-day crossing, Esteban was once again in the scenic mountain valleys of northern Sonora that he remembered so well from his earlier journey with Cabeza de Vaca. Stopping briefly among the friendly Opata Indians, who remembered the strange black shaman from his previous travels, Esteban continued northward and plunged into the second, and much larger, despoblado, located in present-day Arizona. Subdued by the harsh beauty of these desertlands, the caravan pushed on in silence. Somewhere up ahead lay fabulous Cíbola.

Fray Marcos continued his pursuit of Esteban, following the Sonora River to its headwaters and then following the San Pedro River farther northward. Recruiting new porters and guides, he struck out across the desert, moving from watering place to watering place. After 12 days on the despoblado, Fray Marcos's Indian guides informed him that they were drawing near Cíbola. The party quickened its pace and the friar began watching the flat horizon for a sign of the great cities. He had not received any messages from Estéban for several days, but he assumed that Esteban had been welcomed by Cíbola's inhabitants. No doubt the black shaman was comfortably ensconced as the guest of one of the kingdom's rulers. But on May 21, the friar's caravan encountered a frightened, exhausted, badly wounded member of Esteban's retinue. The man was heading in the opposite direction—away from Cíbola. Soon, two more wounded Indians appeared. They related a tale of great woe to Fray Marcos.

About a week before, Esteban's impressive parade had arrived at the first city of Cíbola—the flourishing pueblo of Hawikuh, located in northwest New Mexico and inhabited by the Zuni Indians. With great pomp and supreme self-confidence, Esteban approached the high walls of the pueblo at sunset, announcing himself to the Zuni elders as "a great medicine man and peacemaker." The

Zunis were immediately suspicious of Esteban, and they held a council to discuss the stranger. At best, they all agreed, he was a fool; at worst, a dangerous spy. He was black, which was something they had never seen or even heard of; some of the ornaments he wore marked him as an enemy of the Zunis; he was arrogant and boastful, demanding a tribute of turquoises and Zuni women; and he spoke of "white men" who would come to Hawikuh soon. The Zunis had heard about the white men who had come to the southern lands. They decided to kill this odd "peacemaker." They took Esteban's ornaments, bells, and feathers and soon thereafter filled him with arrows; some of his followers were also killed, whereas the rest scattered and fled. Esteban's corpse was dismembered and distributed among the elders as proof that he was mortal.

Fray Marcos had no plans for martyrdom. Although he later claimed that he pressed on and actually viewed Hawikuh from a distance, more compelling evidence indicates that he listened to the tale of Esteban's demise, turned in his tracks, and went back the way he had come. Despite the heat and the difficult terrain, a series of forced marches—undertaken, as the friar in all honesty wrote later, "with more fear than food"—eventually brought him all the way back to Culiacán by late June 1539. From there, Fray Marcos went to the town of Compostela to report his news to Don Francisco Vázquez de Coronado, governor of the frontier province of New Galicia and a close friend of Viceroy Mendoza's.

Fray Marcos told Coronado about the expedition, Esteban's discovery of the first city of Cíbola, and his own sighting. He assured Coronado that the city Esteban had visited was even greater than Tenochtitlán. Coronado heard the friar's tale, wrote a report to the viceroy on July 15, 1539, and then, taking the friar in hand, set out for Mexico City to personally deliver the details to Mendoza. Although the information was supposed to be top secret, by late August 1539 everybody in Mexico City had heard

Don Antonio de Mendoza, viceroy of New Spain. Mendoza would bankroll the entrada of Coronado. Unlike many of the conquistadores who had first explored the New World—such as the Pizarro brothers and Hernán Cortés—Mendoza insisted on humane treatment of the Native Americans.

about the friar's story—and the story had grown in the telling. The Zuni pueblo discovered by Esteban had been linked to an ancient Spanish legend about seven fabulous cities founded by seven Portuguese bishops who, fleeing an invasion by Muslim armies, had sailed across the Atlantic to the New World. Here at last, perhaps, was El Dorado, that elusive, mythical city of gold that had been drawing Spanish adventurers into the New World since the days of Christopher Columbus. (The legend of El Dorado, which means the golden man, was itself derived from reports about a South American Indian tribe said to anoint its ruler with gold dust.)

As wild speculation and gold fever swept through New Spain, Viceroy Mendoza contemplated his next move. He knew that he had to act quickly, for every conquistador and would-be conquistador in New Spain dreamed of becoming the next Cortés or the new Pizarro, and now Cíbola beckoned to them from the interior. Among the viceroy's potential rivals were Pedro de Alvarado, whose fleet was currently sailing northward along the Pacific Coast of Mexico; Hernando de Soto, who had led an entrada into Florida and who was believed to be moving westward; and the brilliant and ruthless Cortés, the lion

Hernán Cortés (seated), the conquistador who crushed the great Aztec empire, was still prowling about Mexico when Fray Marcos de Niza returned to Mexico City with tales of wondrous Cíbola. Cortés attempted to take control of the subsequent entrada, but his efforts were blocked by Mendoza, and he returned to Spain soon after.

who had crushed the Aztec empire and paved the way for a generation of zealous Spanish adventurers in the New World.

But soon Mendoza's rivals were out of the picture. Alvarado's attention was claimed by an Indian uprising in which he would eventually lose his life, de Soto had vanished into "Florida"—at that time Florida was the name given to a nebulous region stretching westward from the Atlantic Coast—and Cortés had returned to Spain. The wealthy Mendoza began to organize a full-scale entrada to Cíbola. He intended it to be the most well planned, well equipped, and well organized entrada ever, for Mendoza was a careful, thoughtful man, and he had no intention of repeating the mistakes of some of his predecessors. To lead the expedition, Mendoza appointed his young friend, Don Francisco Vázquez de Coronado. The 29-year-old Coronado was given the traditional expeditionary rank of captain-general.

It seemed that Mendoza could not have made a better choice. Born to a noble family in the town of Salamanca in western Spain, Coronado had followed Mendoza to Mexico in 1535 to seek his fortune (the bulk of the Coronado family fortune had gone to Francisco's older brother). Coronado had done well for himself in New Spain. Aided by the patronage of Mendoza, he was appointed to the prestigious council of Mexico City in 1537, and a year later Mendoza made him governor of the province of New Galicia. Within two years of his arrival, Coronado had successfully courted one of the richest and most desirable young women in New Spain—Beatriz de Estrada, the beautiful daughter of the royal treasurer of Spain. Her dowry made Coronado a wealthy man in his own right, providing him with the funds—40 percent of the total cost—he used to help finance the entrada. To his credit, young Coronado had qualities that could not be acquired through patronage or marriage. He was intelligent, discreet, loyal, and even-tempered. He had

The Coronado coat of arms. Like many conquistadores who came to the New World in the 16th century, Coronado was a younger son of a wealthy Spanish family. Virtually disinherited—the family inheritance had gone to an older brother—Coronado was left to his own devices as a young man. Seeking a fortune worthy of the Coronado name, he journeyed to New Spain and married an extremely wealthy woman.

proved his leadership abilities during his service as governor of the wild frontier province of New Galicia. When Mendoza offered him command of the Cíbola entrada, Coronado jumped at the chance, and although he was known as a levelheaded, serious young gentleman, he could not have helped but feel his heart swell with the conquistador's ambition for gold and glory.

The small town of Compostela, located about 500 miles northwest of Mexico City, served as the staging area for Mendoza's entrada. On February 22, 1540, the expeditionary force assembled in the town square. The citizens of Compostela had turned out to watch, and Mendoza himself was present; the viceroy and Coronado observed the proceedings from horseback. Coronado sat his horse proudly, and his fine conquistador's armor, including a gilded helmet with crested plume, flashed in the bright Mexican sunlight. And indeed, the young Spaniard had much to be proud of that day, for he was in command of one of the most impressive entradas ever launched.

Coronado would be leading a total of 337 troops, 226 of whom were mounted. Most of these conquistadores were relatively inexperienced. There were hardened veterans of previous New World entradas, and these men comprised the core of Coronado's force. But a major proportion of the band of adventurers that gathered that day at Compostela were very young men with great aspirations but little experience. Much like Coronado themselves, many of them were the disinherited younger sons of aristocratic Spanish families, and many of them had left behind a frustrating, aimless, and troublesome existence to seek their fortune in the New World. Many were expert caballeros and expert swordsmen. There were quite a few non-Spanish troopers as well—European mercenaries and adventurers, including some Portuguese, Italians, Frenchmen, Germans, and at least one roving Scotsman. The conquistadores carried a variety of weapons—daggers, swords, crossbows, lances, and harquebuses (large, cumbersome, noisy, and often inaccurate muskets).

In addition to these Europeans, the entrada included more than 700 Indians who would serve as servants, scouts, guides, and herdsmen. The herdsmen were needed to supervise the great number of horses brought along by the conquistadores (Coronado alone brought 23 steeds) and the vast herds of sheep and cattle that would provide a mobile source of food during the entrada. (Coronado also hoped to draw supplies from the ships of Spanish naval officer Hernando de Alarcón. These support ships were to sail northward along the Pacific Coast and rendezvous with

(continued on page 32)

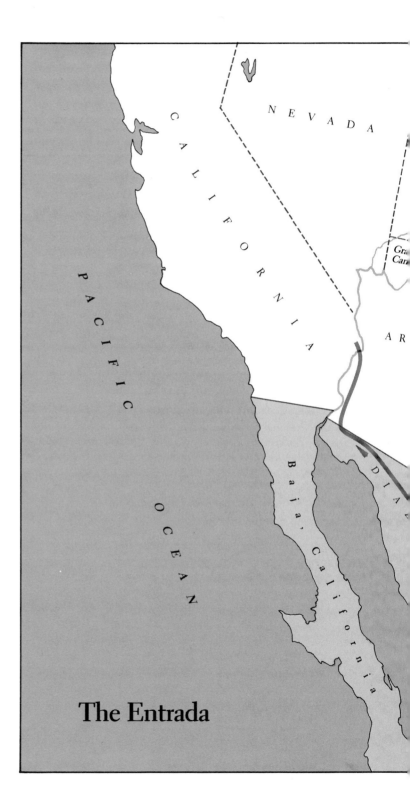

The Entrada

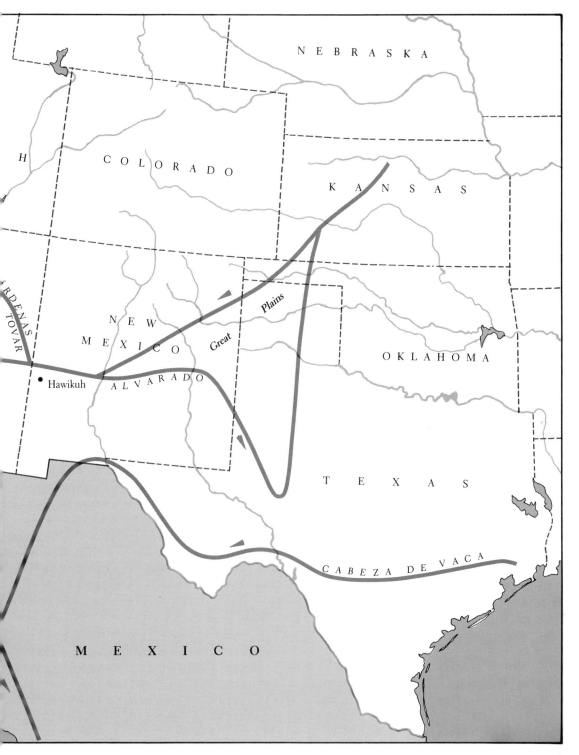

(continued from page 29)
Coronado's party at some point.) A number of black servants—men much like Esteban—accompanied their mas-
ters as well. There were even some women—the wives of
conquistadores as well as the spouses, and in some cases
the children, of lesser members of the party. Ahead of the
procession a contingent of Franciscan priests marched, for
along with the sword, the conquistadores always brought
the cross to those native inhabitants of the New World
they encountered during their entradas. Fray Marcos de

*Coronado leads his company
out of Compostela, Mexico,
on February 22, 1540. The
expeditionary force consisted
of 337 soldiers, 700 Indians, a
contingent of Franciscan priests,
herds of horses and livestock, and
packs of hunting dogs. It was one
of the largest, best-equipped
entradas ever mounted.*

Niza would walk ahead of the priests as guide for the entire expedition.

There was a restless quiet in the town square as one of the priests said mass. After the solemn service, Viceroy Mendoza made an eloquent speech, and the members of the expedition swore a sacred oath of loyalty to their commander, their God, and their king. The following day, with a great clattering of hooves, the last great entrada of the Spanish conquest began.

The Conquest
of Cíbola

From Compostela, Coronado led his expedition north-westward toward the valley of Tepic. On their left, in the distance, the travelers sometimes caught glimpses of blue—the Pacific Ocean. The members of Coronado's caravan gradually adjusted themselves to the rigors of the journey. Admirably, Mendoza had given orders that Indians were not to be exploited as porters—a common practice during entradas—so most of the conquistadores were obliged to carry their own gear. Marching or riding through the *tierra caliente* (hot country)—the lush, tropical Jalisco region of western central Mexico—was hard work, and soon the conquistadores abandoned superfluous possessions in order to lighten their load.

Following a well-known trail and making about 12 miles a day, the expedition continued northward along the verdant coastal plain of Sinaloa. Thickets of tropical brush and pygmy jungle—the *monte*—made the going difficult, and the trail often had to be widened by hand labor. Noisy, colorful flocks of flamingos and parakeets scattered into the air as the Spaniards hacked their way through the brush. As they moved through the coastal foothills and approached the Rio Santiago, the wayfarers refreshed themselves at crystal-clear streams where beautiful spring flowers bloomed. But the alligator-infested Santiago was not so friendly; the entrada was halted as rafts were built

The Hopi pueblo of Walpi, situated atop First Mesa in Arizona. As Coronado's expedition marched through Arizona and New Mexico, they began to make contact with the pueblo-dwelling Native Americans of the Southwest such as the Opatas, the Zunis, and the Hopis. Some of the pueblos were strong enough to resist the armed assaults of the Spaniards.

to ferry people and livestock across. Once across the Rio Santiago, the caravan pushed on to the swift Rio Chiametla and then stopped to rest.

There were two ominous occurrences at the Rio Chiametla in mid-March. First, a party of conquistadores who were out foraging for food encountered a group of hostile Indians. Coronado's camp master and second-in-command, Lope de Samaniego, died instantly when an arrow entered his eye socket and lodged in his brain. Five or six other Spaniards were wounded in the ensuing melee. Not long after this misfortune, the intrepid Captain Melchior Díaz and his tired party of scouts arrived at Coronado's bivouac. Díaz, the former mayor of Culiacán and a trusted member of Mendoza's court, had been sent ahead along the turquoise trail as an advance scout for Coronado's entrada. Both Mendoza and Coronado had hoped that the captain would verify the glowing reports of Fray Marcos de Niza. Díaz had stopped short of Hawikuh during his reconnaissance, but he had seen enough of the surrounding countryside and spoken enough with the local Indians to be skeptical about the presence of gold or treasure of any sort at Cíbola. Díaz had also learned that the Zunis of Hawikuh would not welcome strangers; they still had the bones of poor Esteban on display, and they were ready to receive in a similar manner any intruders—white or black—who might arrive in Esteban's wake.

Despite the pessimistic report of Captain Díaz, Coronado, in true conquistador fashion, moved onward. At Culiacán, he divided his command in order to make better time. He chose about 100 conquistadores and several hundred Indians to form a rapid advance party and ordered the slower main group, with its livestock herds and bulky baggage, to follow at their own pace to Corazones, where they were to establish a base camp. (Corazones, or "Hearts," had acquired its name during the journey of Esteban and Cabeza de Vaca when the local Opata Indians had offered the wanderers 600 dried deer hearts.)

Coronado's vanguard left Culiacán on April 22, 1540, for a rapid advance on Cíbola. They made good progress, soon crossing the Yaquí and Mayo rivers and then passing through some rough country until they reached the first settlements of the Opatas near present-day Ures, Mexico. Like Cabeza de Vaca and Esteban, Coronado was received kindly at Corazones. Resting at the major pueblo of the community, the Spaniards observed their Opata hosts first with curiosity and then with admiration. The Opatas lived well in their extensive agricultural settlements. There were mud and stone houses in the pueblos, temples, and many well tended and irrigated fields of corn, beans, and calabashes, or squashes. They raised turkeys, gathered wild plants, fished, and hunted game to supplement their diet,

In early June 1540, the Spaniards crossed into the present-day United States and passed through the Gila River valley in southern Arizona. Here began the Sonoran despoblados (deserts). "The way is very bad," Coronado wrote as the parched Spaniards labored across the desert.

Coronado's followers, relieved to have survived the first Sonoran despoblado, soon found themselves marching across a second. Many of the conquistadores' horses collapsed and died under the merciless desert sun.

and they fermented an alcoholic drink from cactus plants as well. The Indians also kept domesticated dogs and caged eagles and parrots as pets.

Near the end of May, the Spaniards left the comfort of the Opata settlements and toiled up the scenic gorge of the Sonora River. Following the river's west fork, they advanced onto the northern Sonoran uplands. There, the expedition entered the present-day United States at a point in Arizona near the town of Palominas. They then followed the San Pedro River downstream to the Gila River valley of southern Arizona. They were now passing through a strange, prehistoric landscape. Some of the valley's creosote bushes are known to be more than 11,000 years old. To their left as they marched were the Huachuca Mountains, dotted with ancient bristlecone pines. To their right were the dry Mule Mountains.

Pausing briefly at the Gila River, Coronado led his troops through a pass in the Winchester Mountains and followed an Indian trail to some ruins called Chichilticale, or Red House, so named because it was built of red mud. They bivouacked here, for the men were tired. They were also hungry. Coronado sorely needed to be resupplied by Alarcón's ships, but he had no idea where—or how far away—the ocean was. (Had he known, he would have no doubt been appalled.) The growling stomachs of the travelers added a new sense of urgency to the entrada. Ahead lay the despoblado.

"To vary our past tribulations we found no grass during the first days and encountered more dangerous passages than we had previously experienced. The horses were so exhausted they could not endure it, and, in this last desert, we lost more than previously. The way is very bad . . . ." Thus, in a letter to Mendoza, did Coronado describe the grueling 150-mile trek across the despoblado that June of 1540. But once they reached the Natanes Plateau they had put the Sonoran Desert to their rear. Now they found themselves in country that seemed heavenly compared with the parched despoblado—the Black River region at the southern edge of the magnificent Mogollon forests of Arizona. The Spaniards rode briskly through cool, shadowy glens and woodlands and crossed the White River on rafts, not far from Lake Mountain. But a new misfortune awaited them near the end of this hospitable pine forest. Driven by hunger, a Spaniard and two black servants devoured a species of poisonous wild plant, probably *Cicuta douglasii* (also known as water hemlock), and died in agony soon after. They were buried in shallow graves in a spot referred to afterward by the Spanish as the Camp of Death.

After burying their dead companions, the party moved down off the Natanes Plateau into open country. Coronado sent one of his most trusted captains, Don García López de Cárdenas, to ride forward as a scout. Ahead lay the distant mesas of the Colorado Plateau, including the stark, forbidding *Towaya' lane* (Corn Mountain), regarded as sacred by the Zunis. Several toilsome days later the expedition reached the muddy, reddish waters of the Rio Vermejo (Red River), known today as the Little Colorado River. Here, the ever-hungry conquistadores were delighted to catch fish that resembled those found in Spain's rivers.

The expedition was getting close to its goal. Cárdenas, riding with 15 caballeros ahead of the main body of troops,

encountered the first Cíbolans. Two of the Indians were kept as "guests," and two others were sent homeward with a cross and instructions to await the Spaniards. Advancing toward Hawikuh along the Zuni River, the captain-general and his men observed columns of smoke from signal fires appearing from point to point, and they suspected that they were being followed and watched. Their suspicions

The flotilla of Spanish mariner Hernando de Alarcón, laden with supplies for Coronado's entrada, sailed down the Pacific Coast to the Sea of Cortés and the mouth of the Colorado River, where Alarcón waited—in vain—for word from the captain-general.

were confirmed by a midnight ambush along the Zuni
River. A number of screaming Indians rushed out of the
night and assaulted the camp of Cárdenas. After a vigorous
defense by the conquistadores, the natives melted back
into the darkness. This was the first warlike encounter
between Europeans and Native Americans in the American Southwest. There were no casualties, but the Spaniards were clearly unnerved, for they named the spot Bad
Pass before moving on.

The riders at the front of the caravan now crossed open,
grassy plains under the expansive southwestern skies. Coronado drew up with Cárdenas as Hawikuh came into
sight. Cíbola at last! The Zuni pueblo rose up out of the
plain as the conquistadores approached. The Zunis were
ready for them; hundreds of Indian warriors poured out
of the pueblo, ready to defend their city. They blew great
blasts on war horns, shouted threats and taunts, lit grass
fires, collected stones for throwing, and prepared their
arrows and clubs. Several of them drew a long line with
cornmeal on the ground in front of Hawikuh. The message
was clear—to cross the line meant death.

The conquistadores reined in their horses and came to
a halt. The two armies, representing two vastly different
cultures, faced each other. The Spaniards sized up the
Zunis, and the Indians looked with wonder at the armored
Spanish troops and their powerful war-horses. They had
never seen or heard of horses before, and they had no idea
what these monstrous, galloping creatures were. Coronado
directed Captain Cárdenas, two Franciscans, a notary, and
a small armed escort to approach the Zunis. They moved
forward cautiously, and the notary launched into a speech,
announcing the Spaniards' intention of claiming Cíbola
for God and king. The Zunis listened to the long-winded
Spaniard for a while and then let loose a volley of arrows.
The emissaries turned around and rode back to the main
force. Coronado spoke a quiet word with the priests, re-

questing the official sanction of the Catholic church before he attacked. The priests nodded. Coronado spurred his horse, rode to the front, raised his sword, and shouted the traditional conquistador battle cry—"*Santiago-y-a-ellos!*" (For St. James and at them!) The Spaniards charged with a roar and the battle of Hawikuh was on.

The Zuni line of defense quickly wilted, for there was nothing so terrifying as a massed charge of Spanish cavalry. Those Indians who did not make it to the safety of the pueblo's walls were ridden down and slain by the Spaniards. The conquistadores then regrouped and charged the pueblo itself. Crossbowmen and harquebusiers opened fire as Coronado led an assault on a small entryway.

The Zunis mounted a stiff defense from the high walls of their citadel, raining arrows and large rocks down on the invaders. Openly marked as a leader by his gilded armor and plumed helmet, Coronado was the focus of an intense battering as the Spaniards fought their way into Hawikuh. Twice he was knocked down by heavy rocks; the second barrage rendered the captain-general senseless. Two of his captains, shielding his prostrate body with their own, dragged him to safety while the battle raged on without him.

The fight was over by the time Coronado regained consciousness. The Zunis, overwhelmed by the Spaniards, had fled, abandoning their pueblo to the invaders. The conquest of the first city of Cíbola was complete! But it was a rude awakening for the captain-general nevertheless, for he was bruised and battered from head to toe and in great pain. Even more troubling were the expressions his men wore as they investigated the interior of Hawikuh. The conquistadores were visibly disgruntled, and many of them muttered and cursed. This first great city of legendary Cíbola was nothing like the place Fray Marcos had described. Although the multileveled pueblo was impressive architecturally, it contained no gold, no silver, no jewels,

no riches. Fray Marcos had exaggerated. The angry conquistadores put it less kindly: The priest had lied. They cursed him roundly, and some of them were in favor of cutting off his head on the spot. Coronado summed up the situation in a letter to Mendoza: "To make a long story short, I can assure you that [Fray Marcos] has not told the truth in a single thing he has said."

Despite his disappointment and his aching head, the captain-general remained hopeful and positive in his out-

Coronado's troops launched an attack on the Zuni pueblo of Hawikuh on July 7, 1540. The Zuni warriors rained stones and arrows down on the conquistadores, knocking Coronado, who led the charge, unconscious. But the swords and guns of the Spaniards eventually prevailed, and the Zunis were forced to abandon their home to the invaders.

look. He had not conquered a New Peru like Pizarro, or toppled a rich empire like Cortés, but he was alive and his army was virtually intact. And Hawikuh did have something that the Spanish sorely needed—food supplies. While he lay recuperating, his hungry men prepared a great feast from the captured stores of maize, beans, and turkeys. The Zunis, Coronado wrote with some satisfaction to Mendoza later, made "the best tortillas that I have ever seen anywhere."

Coronado's Captains

After the battle of Hawikuh, the Spaniards rested. Occupying the abandoned pueblo, they ate hearty meals from the Zunis' abundant stores of food, cut hay for their tired and hungry horses, and examined their strange new quarters. Coronado gave strict orders for humane treatment of the vanquished Zunis and during the next few weeks took pains to placate the Indians. Gifts were presented and the Zuni chiefs were received by Coronado with due ceremony. In return for peace, Coronado required the Zunis to acknowledge the Christian God and the king of Spain. Although they remained deeply suspicious of their new overlords, a few Zunis gradually drifted back to their settlements.

By mid-July 1540, the captain-general had recovered sufficiently from his battle wounds to explore the surrounding countryside and neighboring settlements, including Matsaki, the Zuni pueblo on Corn Mountain mesa. In a letter to Viceroy Mendoza, Coronado described the area and its inhabitants. The Zunis, he wrote, were "fairly large" and "quite intelligent." The summer climate in Cíbola was similar to that of Mexico, but Coronado suspected that the winters were very cold. "There are many animals here," he also noted, including "bears, tigers [bobcats], lions [cougars], porcupines, and some sheep [elk] as big as horses, with large horns and little tails." There were

Hernando de Alvarado, one of Coronado's trusted captains, led a reconnaissance party to the region known as Tiguex, on the banks of the Rio Grande, in September 1540. Alvarado found Tiguex to be so hospitable that he advised Coronado to move his entire force there for the winter.

also wild goats, peccaries, deer, and he had seen many tanned skins of the "cattle"—buffalo—of the plains region to the east.

Coronado's letter to Mendoza also detailed the conquistador's plans for his entrada now that Cíbola had been conquered: "I have decided to send men throughout all the surrounding regions in order to find out if there is anything worthwhile; to suffer every hardship rather than abandon this enterprise; and to serve his Majesty if I can find any way to do so." Accordingly, the captain-general began to send his most capable captains on a series of missions that together would result in the first major reconnaissance of the American Southwest.

The Zunis had volunteered information about a province called Tusayan located northwest of Hawikuh. For several centuries, the Spaniards were told, the people of Tusayan had traded goods with the Zunis. On July 15, 1540, Coronado dispatched Captain Pedro de Tovar, the tough Franciscan Fray Juan de Padilla, and a small armed escort to the northwest with orders to locate and explore Tusayan. Following several Zuni guides along an ancient trade route, Tovar's party rode through the desolate but spectacular country of eastern Arizona. Traveling from water hole to water hole, they passed Navajo Springs, skirted the Petrified Forest, and entered the Jeddito Valley from the east. They were now in the land of the Hopituh, "the peaceful people," whose descendants are known as the Hopis.

Tovar and his men encountered the first Hopi settlement—Awatowi—on an evening in late July. Above them, on Antelope Mesa, they could hear the Indians "talking in their houses." Quietly, the Spaniards made camp. They awoke the next morning to find themselves confronted by Hopi warriors. As at Hawikuh, Indian shamans advanced to draw lines in the earth with sacred cornmeal. Other warriors yelled and danced their defiance and brandished their wooden war clubs, shields, and bows.

Tiring of the standoff, the Spaniards charged the Hopis, who broke and fled before the furious and terrifying horsemen. A number of warriors were slain before the routed Hopis sued for peace and offered gifts to Captain Tovar.

Word of the terrible strangers quickly spread throughout Tusayan, and soon emissaries from nearby pueblos came to render obeisance. Tovar and his men were allowed to tour the province in peace. West of Awatowi were four more large pueblos—Walpi, Mishongnovi, Shongopovi, and Oraibi. All of these sky cities were perched high above the surrounding plains on giant Black Mesa. There, be-

Coronado quickly recovered from the wounds he received at Hawikuh and was soon back in the saddle. During the summer of 1540 he toured the province of Cíbola, visiting the pueblos and making peace with their Zuni inhabitants.

As they traveled through the Southwest, the Spaniards encountered many animals they had never seen before. Their descriptions of these creatures resulted in artistic portrayals such as this one.

neath the blue dome of the southwestern skies, the usually peaceful Hopis tended their fields, raised cotton, and produced wonderful weavings to barter along the trade routes.

Captain Tovar was impressed with the Hopis. They were an industrious, religious, and artistic people. But as he rode through the province from pueblo to pueblo and questioned the Indians, Tovar learned that they had no gold and little else of great value to the Spaniards. The reconnaissance party was back at Hawikuh by mid-August, and the captain reported his findings to Coronado. One part of Tovar's unremarkable account of the journey caught Coronado's attention. The Hopis had spoken to Tovar about a "great river" to the west. On this enormous river, according to the Indians, lived a race of giants.

The captain-general listened intently to this talk of a great river to the west. About a year before, a Spanish mariner named Francisco de Ulloa, exploring the Gulf of California, had seen the mouth of a large river (what would come to be known as the Colorado River) that snaked away inland. Before he had launched his entrada, Coronado had made plans to rendezvous with the ships of sea captain Hernando de Alarcón somewhere along the coast. If, by chance, Alarcón reached Ulloa's river before he made his connection with Coronado, he was to follow the river inland as far as possible. Perhaps, Coronado now surmised, the great river the Hopis had spoken of to Tovar was Ulloa's river. If that was so, Alarcón and his supplies might be on the river at that very moment.

Coronado wasted no time in acting on this information. He immediately dispatched another reconnaissance sortie, this one consisting of 25 horsemen under the command of one of his finest captains, Don García López de Cárdenas. They were to retrace Captain Tovar's route to Tusayan and then proceed westward to the alleged "great river" and, hopefully, Alarcón's ships. Cárdenas was given 80 days to complete his mission. The captain and his men

(continued on page 54)

Oraibi, the Hopi pueblo situated atop Third Mesa in northern Arizona. Oraibi survived the coming of the conquistadores and today is thought to be one of the oldest continually inhabited towns in North America.

The Unvanquished

In Mexico, conquistador Hernán Cortés encountered the mighty Aztec empire. In Peru, Pizarro found the great Inca domain. Coronado also came to grips with an advanced Indian culture—that of the pueblo-dwelling Indians of the American Southwest (known collectively as the Pueblo Indians).

Pueblo is Spanish for "town"; the Spaniards used this term for Indians such as the Zuni and the Hopi because they lived in towns—remarkable apartment complexes made of adobe bricks, often multistoried and built atop towering mesas. And although the various Pueblo tribes of Coronado's time had no formal political structure binding the separate city-states together, they were capable of forming a cohesive alliance when necessary, as they did in the 1680 revolt against Mexico. And at one time (about five centuries before Coronado) the Pueblo tribes had all been part of a sprawling, loosely connected network of settlements that might be characterized as a nation of sorts. The hub of this flourishing civilization was Chaco Canyon, New Mexico, where the largest pueblo of all—a giant adobe hive—was located.

The Aztec and the Incas are gone now; anthropologists and archaeologists have only fragments of their cultures to study. But the Pueblo civilization—with its culture and history relatively intact—perseveres. Indeed, the Pueblo Indians are among the tribes of Native Americans that have been the most successful in maintaining their traditional "lifeways"—and thus their sense of cultural well-being—through the years.

Why has the Pueblo culture survived while other, more powerful, Native American civilizations have all but vanished? The answer, perhaps, can be found within the Pueblo culture itself. The Pueblo Indians adhere to a peaceful way of life in which communal well-being and harmony are cherished and rewarded, whereas personal ambition and displays of excess individuality are frowned upon. Moderation, not excess, is admired, and the qualities of modesty and inoffensiveness are held above all others. These aspects of Pueblo culture provide it with an inner strength, a center that holds together even under great stress. Although the Pueblo Indians were defeated militarily, they have yet to be overwhelmed or undermined culturally.

A Hopi pueblo at Shongopovi village in Arizona, which is still occupied today.

(continued from page 51)

left Hawikuh on August 25 and followed Tovar's route to Tusayan, where the party rested a bit before pushing westward behind a number of Hopi guides.

Twenty days of rough and thirsty travel through uninhabited country brought the expedition across the Coconino Plateau. Suddenly, moving through an elevated landscape of twisted pines, the Spaniards were forced to pull their horses up short, for ahead of them, with little warning whatsoever, the ground had vanished. Cautiously, the Spaniards dismounted and moved forward, coming to the edge of an unimaginable abyss. They were thus the first Europeans to see Arizona's awe-inspiring Grand Canyon. The men marveled speechlessly at the chasm, which was so immense it played tricks on their eyes. Gazing at the ribbon of water far below—the Colorado River—the Spaniards thought it was a smallish stream about six feet wide or so. Their Hopi guides, however, assured them that the river was more than a mile wide!

For three days, Captain Cárdenas and his men explored the south rim of the canyon, trying to find a safe route down to the river below, for the captain believed that this must be the great river spoken of by the Hopis. On the morning of the third day, three brave and agile Spaniards attempted the descent. They lowered themselves over the rim and were soon lost to sight. Their *compañeros* waited nervously for the return of the fledgling rock climbers. Just before nightfall, the three exhausted, scraped, and dusty Spaniards hauled themselves up over the rim. They said that they had been down about a third of the way and that the river seemed very large from that vantage point—as large as their Hopi guides had claimed.

The canyon made for splendid scenery, but for Captain Cárdenas it proved to be a frustrating—and ultimately insurmountable—obstacle. As he prowled westward for four days, the days grew shorter and the nights grew colder. Supplies began to run out, and the Hopi guides advised

Cárdenas to turn back, as there was no water ahead. Finally, the captain admitted defeat—a bitter admission for any conquistador—and the party began the long retreat to Hawikuh.

After sending Cárdenas westward, Coronado had turned his attention to the south. Earlier in the entrada, the slow-moving bulk of Coronado's force had been left behind at Culiacán. From there, they had proceeded to the Opata

A reconnaissance party led by Captain García López de Cárdenas arrived at the south rim of the Grand Canyon in September 1540. The conquistadores were rendered speechless by the awesome gorge.

settlements at Corazones, where, under the command of
Captain Tristán de Arellano, they had established a base
camp. Coronado now decided to call them forward to
Hawikuh. For this task he chose his most experienced
scout, Captain Melchior Díaz. Once he had delivered
Coronado's orders to Arellano, Díaz was to lead an expedition to the southwest, toward the Pacific Coast, in a
renewed attempt to link up with Alarcón. Along with Díaz
went several dozen soldiers, couriers bearing Coronado's

letters to Mendoza, and Fray Marcos. The discredited friar· was being sent home for his own good, for many of the conquistadores still expressed an urge to chop off his tonsured head.

Díaz and company arrived at Corazones in mid-September 1540. Fray Marcos, with a small escort, continued on to Mexico City, while Díaz helped Arellano prepare for the march to Hawikuh. By the end of the month, all but 80 soldiers were on their way to join Coronado, and

The junction of the Gila and Colorado rivers in Yuma, Arizona. In this region, Captain Melchior Díaz encountered a "race of giants"—the Yuman Indians, many of whom were reportedly more than seven feet tall.

Díaz was ready to continue the search for the ships of Alarcón. With some two dozen Spaniards and several Indian guides, he struck out for the terra incognita northwest of the Sonora Valley. They rode through the country of the Pima and Papago Indians along some of the fiercest desert trails in the greater Southwest; some historians believe they might have traveled the infamous Camino del Diablo (Devil's Highway).

The countryside of present-day Yuma, Arizona, around the lower Colorado River, offered the explorers a welcome contrast to the desert lands they had crossed. The big, sediment-laden river (called Rio del Tizon, or Firebrand River, by the Spanish because of the local Indians' habit of carrying torches to warm themselves) flowed sluggishly across a flat, fertile landscape of fields and little settlements of semisubterranean grass huts. Even more amazing were the remarkably tall and strong Yuman Indians—here were the "giants" that the Hopis had spoken of—who astounded the Spaniards with their size, strength, and endurance. One of these Indians reportedly hoisted and carried a log that six Spaniards had been unable to budge.

As he moved along the Colorado, Díaz was told by the Indians that small Spanish-style launches had been seen downstream. These could be only Alarcón's men, Díaz realized, and he quickened the pace of his march along the river.

Three days later he made a startling and improbable discovery. Carved in a tree on the riverbank, in Spanish, was a message from Alarcón: "Alarcón came this far. There are letters at the foot of this tree." Díaz dug up the buried letters with haste. Reading them, he learned that Captain Alarcón had come upriver as far as possible and then had waited for word from Coronado. But hearing nothing from the captain-general, he had returned to the main flotilla in the Gulf of California. (Baja California, the letter noted, was not an island, as supposed, but a great peninsula.)

The date on the letters told Díaz that he had missed linking up with Alarcón by only two months.

Alarcón's letters marked the beginning of a period of bad luck—and ultimately disaster—for Díaz. His supplies were running low, and the local Indians were becoming less than hospitable. After fighting off an attack, the Spanish constructed rafts from bundles of reeds and crossed the river. On the far side, Díaz and his men pushed onward until they reached the arid lands around the Mojave Mountains, thus becoming the first Europeans to enter present-day California. There, they encountered hot springs and mud volcanoes "like something infernal."

Not long after crossing into California, Díaz found himself caught in his own personal hell. Out riding one day, he accidently impaled himself on a lance he had just hurled at a disobedient pet greyhound. The shaft of the weapon penetrated his groin and ruptured his bladder. Captain Díaz held grimly to life as his men made a forced march back toward Corazones. Despite the desperate efforts of his fellow conquistadores, Díaz succumbed to his wound and died on January 18, 1541. He was buried in "a wild place," and the site of his grave remains unknown.

While Coronado's captains were engaged in their explorations, word of the fierce, bearded aliens and their monstrous animals spread outward from Hawikuh along the aboriginal trade routes of the Southwest. Some Indians were more curious than frightened, however, and late in the summer of 1540 a party of inquisitive Native Americans from the east arrived at Hawikuh to see for themselves the strange newcomers. These travelers had walked some 300 miles to Hawikuh from Cicuye, their pueblo on the Pecos River in eastern New Mexico. They were led by two intelligent and sociable men to whom the Spaniards immediately took a liking. The two Indians were given Spanish nicknames. Bigotes (Whiskers) was a handsome young chief, and Cacique (Governor) was a pueblo elder.

Coronado questioned Bigotes and Cacique about their homelands and listened with growing interest as the two Indians described the rivers, strong towns, and especially the herds of buffalo in the east. Clearly, an eastern reconnaissance was called for, and on August 29, 1540, Captain Hernando de Alvarado rode out from Hawikuh at the head of a company of 20 men, including Bigotes and Cacique, who volunteered to act as guides.

Bigotes and Cacique quickly proved to be more than simply guides. The two men functioned as cross-cultural diplomats and interpreters, smoothing the passage of the Spaniards through the communities of the Tiwas, Keras, and Towas they encountered as they moved eastward across New Mexico. After 75 miles of travel through the wild *malpais* (badlands) of dwarf piñon and dried lava near

the Continental Divide, Alvarado's party reached the impressive pueblo of Acoma. They paused to marvel at this sky city, a seemingly impregnable Indian citadel built high atop a lonely mesa. (Acoma still stands today, one of the oldest continually inhabited towns in the United States.) On September 7, the party arrived on the banks of the Rio Grande. With Bigotes and Cacique traveling ahead as peace emissaries, the Spaniards passed unmolested through the fertile Rio Grande valley and the many agrarian towns of the local Tiwa Indians. The Spaniards dubbed this region Tiguex.

Captain Alvarado was greatly impressed by Tiguex. Clearly, these lands offered more food resources than the Zuni lands. Irrigated fields of maize, beans, and squashes blanketed the lands on either side of the river, supporting

The fertile country around New Mexico's Rio Grande provided the Tiwa Indians with a pleasant homeland. Coronado and his troops arrived in this region— known as Tiguex—in the fall of 1540 and settled in for a long and bloody winter.

about 80 pueblos. The valley also featured pleasant cottonwood groves and plenty of good water. The Tiwas and the other Indians seemed friendly enough, "more given to farming," noted Alvarado, "than to war." The captain sent a map and a report back to Hawikuh, strongly urging Coronado to relocate his main force to this promising land.

Alvarado then continued his reconnaissance, moving in an easterly direction to the fortress pueblo of Cicuye, located on a low mesa overlooking the Pecos River near Glorieta Pass. A major Tano population center, Cicuye acted as a funnel for trade products, such as buffalo robes, passing back and forth between the eastern plains and the western pueblos. Like Acoma, Cicuye was also a defensive stronghold, with walls and terraces soaring up to five stories high.

Bigotes and Cacique were popular and honored citizens, and their safe return was duly celebrated with drum and flute music. The Spaniards were welcomed as guests and invited to stay and rest, but Alvarado was pressed for time and anxious to continue his mission. He asked Bigotes to continue onward with them on the trek eastward to the buffalo plains, but the chief declined and offered two of his slaves to Alvarado instead. Called Sopete and El Turco (the Turk, because of his resemblance to one) by the Spaniards, these men were captives from the plains and were familiar with routes to the east.

With the two new guides pointing the way, Alvarado's company traveled southeast from Cicuye, and then due east. On the horizon before them loomed an enormous plateau, one of the world's largest and flattest plains—the Llano Estacado (Staked Plains), as later travelers called it. Here, the Spaniards finally encountered the thunderous herds of the great shaggy beasts they had heard so much about—the buffalo. "The country," one Spaniard observed, "was covered with them." The Spaniards at first had trouble killing the beasts, hacking at them fruitlessly with their swords while their horses were disemboweled

East of the Rio Grande, the Spaniards encountered their first buffalo. More than 60 million of the "monstrous beasts" rumbled over the American plains in the 16th century. They were as numerous, one Spaniard wrote, as "the fish of the sea." Seen here is the earliest known European depiction of the buffalo.

by the buffaloes' horns. But soon, using lances, the conquistadores became adept at buffalo hunting, and they found the meat of this animal to be quite tasty.

It was out on the buffalo plains one day that El Turco began to relate to Alvarado, using sign language, an account of a bountiful kingdom to the northwest. He called the place Quivira and assured the Spaniards that there was much gold and silver there. According to El Turco, Bigotes possessed proof of the riches of Quivira—a wonderful golden bracelet. Predictably, this information created a major sensation among the ever-greedy conquistadores. Alvarado and his men immediately turned around and headed back for Cicuye. They were particularly anxious to interrogate Bigotes about the alleged golden bracelet.

The events that followed were tragic. At Cicuye, both Bigotes and Cacique claimed to know nothing about a golden bracelet. They said El Turco was lying. Moreover, they refused to travel to Tiguex, where Coronado had set up a new base camp on the Rio Grande, to discuss the matter. Alvarado then had the four Indians who had acted as guides—Bigotes, Cacique, Sopete, and El Turco— bound with chains. They were then subjected to a humiliating march back to Tiguex. Confident that he was on the brink of wealth and good fortune, Captain Alvarado had instead become the catalyst for great misfortune.

The Tiguex War

As soon as he could, Coronado had acted on Alvarado's recommendation to relocate the main force of his army from Hawikuh to the Tiguex pueblos along the Rio Grande. The captain-general had established his new camp in Tiguex by late November 1540, and soon afterward Alvarado arrived with his prisoners and tales of the "kingdom" of Quivira. Alvarado brought El Turco before Coronado and the Indian repeated his story about Quivira's riches. Coronado, like most of the conquistadores, was surprisingly gullible when it came to stories of great golden cities in the New World, and soon the captain-general and his entire camp were in a ferment.

Bigotes, still in chains, was brought before Coronado and questioned about the golden bracelet that El Turco had talked about. The chief from Cicuye was a proud and honorable man, and he denied, in all honesty, any knowledge of a golden bracelet or gold in general. El Turco, he said, was a liar. The conquistadores, who were also capable of endless cruelties when it came to the subject of gold in the New World, then took Bigotes to a field outside the encampment and set their savage dogs upon him. Still Bigotes maintained his innocence.

The Tiwas observed these events with a growing uneasiness; the Spaniards' treatment of Bigotes, who was, after all, a chief, was a bad sign. As winter crept over the New

New World conquistadores were frequently guilty of savage mistreatment of Native Americans, many of whom were pressed into slavery as porters. During the winter of 1540–41, Coronado's men resorted to similar behavior, which led to war with the Indians of Tiguex.

Coronado moved the bulk of his force from Hawikuh to Tiguex just as the first snows of winter arrived in New Mexico. It did not take long for the Spaniards to wear out their welcome at the Rio Grande pueblos.

Mexico landscape and the Rio Grande began to freeze over, so did relations between the Spaniards and the Indians. The nature of Coronado's entrada began to change. Until then, the captain-general and his men had behaved in a relatively benevolent manner, as compared to the blood-soaked entradas of previous conquistadores such as the Pizarros. But now Coronado and his men became invaders—and ultimately, destroyers—rather than explorers.

In mid-December the Tiwas were told to abandon one of their larger pueblos—called Alcanfor—so that the Spaniards could take up residence there for the remainder of the winter. As the winter wore on, the conquistadores became increasingly contemptuous of the Indians. Food and clothing were routinely taken from them without recompense, and the warriors of Tiguex grew restless. When an Indian woman was raped by one of the Spaniards, the Tiwas had had enough. War broke out on the banks of the Rio Grande.

The Tiwas initiated open hostilities with a raid on a corral where the Spaniards kept their horses. The horses were stampeded and many of them were killed by Tiwa arrows. The Spaniards responded with typical conquistador fury. Led by Captain Cárdenas, they launched a full-scale attack on the pueblo of Arenal, where the Indians had gathered. A bitter struggle ensued as the Spaniards stormed the Tiwa stronghold. The Indians mounted a fierce defense, but the conquistadores used their swords, crossbows, and muskets to penetrate the pueblo. The battle raged anew the next morning within Arenal, with the Spaniards hacking and blasting their way from room to room and the Tiwas falling back toward the center of the pueblo. Cárdenas ordered fires set, and the desperate Tiwas emerged and began to flee in disorder. Out in the open, they were easily run down by mounted Spaniards. Many Indians surrendered; those who did not were cut down as they ran. A good number of the captive Tiwas were then burned alive by Coronado's men, and their horrible shrieks filled the cold air as the sun went down. By the end of that bloody day, Arenal was a smoking ruin and hundreds of Tiwas were dead.

Although the resistance at Arenal had been crushed, the conquistadores' blood was up. As the mounted soldiers rampaged through the fields and villages, the Tiwas retreated to another defensible pueblo, called Moho, and prepared to make a final stand. It was not long before Coronado's entire force fell on the pueblo. The Tiwas within put up a stubborn and valiant resistance. Unable to fight their way into Moho, the conquistadores settled in for a siege. After 50 desperate days, the starving and thirsty Indians decided to try and fight their way through the encirclement. Just before dawn on a freezing day in March, the warriors charged out of the pueblo. The Spaniards were briefly surprised, but they quickly rallied. The Tiwas' surprise attack became a panicked rout. As the Indians fled for the river, the conquistadores rode them down mercilessly. Some of the Tiwas reached the icy Rio Grande and swam to safety, but many others were put to the sword, drowned, or enslaved.

By the end of March, Coronado had stamped out any remaining resistance in Tiguex. Hundreds of Indians had been killed, and 12 major pueblos had been smashed. The Indians, for their part, now regarded the Spaniards as a race of fiends. If Coronado felt any misgivings about these unfortunate events, he did not show it, for as soon as the spring thaw began he turned his attention to the east.

During the long siege of Moho, Coronado and his captains diverted themselves by listening to El Turco describe the marvels of Quivira, a land supposedly so rich that the "lord of that country took his afternoon nap under a great tree on which were hung a great number of little gold bells, which put him to sleep as they swung in the air." Bigotes continued to maintain that El Turco was lying— the chief from Cicuye was still in chains but the Spaniards had given up torturing him, for he could not be broken— but although many of the conquistadores did not trust El

A thunderous charge by mounted conquistadores was one of the most awe-inspiring and intimidating aspects of 16th-century warfare. For the Native Americans of the Southwest, who had never seen horses before— never mind mounted warriors—it was a particularly frightening experience.

Turco, they all wanted to believe in the existence of another El Dorado. Coronado, hoping that gold and glory
awaited him on the buffalo plains, began preparing to
renew his entrada, and by April 23, 1541, the Spaniards
were ready to move eastward.

The conquistadores presented an impressive sight on
that spring morning as they waited for the captain-general
to give them the order to move out. They were swelled
with their victory over the Tiwas, and their confidence
and hopes were high. Their horses were sleek and frisky,
their armor was newly cleaned and shined brightly in the
sun, and the colorful pennons attached to their lances
flapped and waved in the stiff breeze. They rode out of
Tiguex proudly and moved eastward into the rising sun.
The surviving Tiwas were no doubt happy to see their
backs.

The expedition moved eastward at a leisurely pace,
reaching Cicuye and the Pecos River by the end of April.
There, Coronado gathered additional provisions for the
journey. He also released Bigotes and Cacique to their
own people. El Turco, who had courted the captain-
general's favor all winter, was made the primary guide for
the trek to Quivira.

The Spaniards left Cicuye on May 1 and headed southeast, following the Pecos River. A few days later, probably
in the vicinity of present-day Puerto de Luna, New Mexico, they decided to cross the river, which was running
high and fast from spring rains and the thawing of mountain snows. For four days the men labored to build a bridge
across the turbulent waters, after which they engaged in
the arduous task of getting themselves and their livestock
and other supplies to the other side.

Some 100 miles after fording the Pecos, Coronado's
expedition would pass from present-day New Mexico into
Texas. The Spaniards, of course, were oblivious of these
future boundaries, but they were aware that upon crossing
the river they had arrived in new terra incognita. Ahead

lay the ramparts of the Llano Estacado; beyond that the lands flattened out and stretched away unbroken to the horizon. Once their horses had clambered up onto this elevated tableland, the conquistadores halted at the edge of this ocean of grasslands and gazed at it in wonder, for—aside from Alvarado's company—none of them had seen anything like it before. For them, the utter flatness and the seemingly infinite dimensions of this land were overwhelming. "There, things were remarkable" one Spaniard wrote. Coronado himself wrote that there was "not a stone, not a bit of rising ground, not a tree, not a shrub, not anything." Nevertheless, the conquistadores harbored no thoughts of turning back, and soon they were riding into the Great Plains.

From Tiguex, Coronado led his force eastward, toward the land of Quivira. But the bewildered Spaniards soon found themselves adrift on a seemingly endless ocean of grasslands—the Great Plains.

Quest for Quivira

As Coronado's company pushed into the llano, the land seemed to encircle them. "The country is like a bowl," one of them wrote, "so that when a man sits down, the horizon surrounds him all around." Traveling over this endless prairie was like voyaging at sea, and the Spaniards became confused and disoriented, beset by mirages and other optical illusions. Strangers in a strange land, they wandered aimlessly across the flat countryside, a procession of bewildered, once-proud warriors. Men who were sent away from the main column to hunt or scout sometimes lost all sense of direction and could not find their way back. The conquistadores rode about, blowing trumpets and shooting off their guns, hoping that those who were lost would be guided back to safety by the sounds. If it was nighttime, they built fires as beacons. Sometimes, lost men would straggle back into camp, wild-eyed and starving. Sometimes they would not.

Soon the Spaniards entered what they called "the domain of the cows"—the summer grazing grounds for the huge buffalo herds of the plains. They were astounded by the sheer numbers of buffalo—there were millions of them. Indeed, the shaggy beasts were omnipresent. "There was not a single day until my return that I lost sight of them," Coronado wrote. To the Europeans, their appearance was as startling as their great numbers. One Spaniard described them in this manner: They had "very long beards like goats," woolly hair "like a sheep's," tails

In the spring of 1541, Coronado led his caballeros and missionaries across the buffalo plains of Texas. In late May they arrived at the Red River barrancas, where they rested among the Teyas Indians before pushing on toward Kansas.

"like a scorpion," a big hump "larger than a camel's," and they shed their hair around the middle, "which [made] perfect lions of them." The Spaniards were not so awed by the beasts that they were afraid of them, however, and eventually they all became expert buffalo hunters. At one point later on in their travels, they killed more than 500 bulls during a two-week period, giving them a steady supply of buffalo meat.

Wandering through the fog one summer morning, several of Coronado's scouts observed strange markings on the ground, as if someone had dragged lances across the plains. The scouts followed the markings, which eventually brought them to a small, curious encampment of Indians. These were the Querechos, the nomadic plains Indians, ancestors of the Apaches. The Querechos reminded the Spaniards of the nomadic Arab tribesmen of

As they crossed the plains, the Spaniards never lost sight of the buffalo. They killed the animals in large numbers, thus beginning the process of extermination that would end in the late 19th century with the virtual extinction of the great herds.

Coronado and his men were intrigued by the wandering Native Americans of the plains, who used dogs as beasts of burden. These nomads had a symbiotic relationship with the buffalo, and they followed the herds from place to place.

the North African deserts. The strange markings they had followed to the encampment had been caused by the dogs that the Querechos used to drag their tipi poles and other belongings from one campsite to another.

As the main column of Coronado's force slowly arrived in the vicinity of their little village, the Indians showed neither fear nor much interest in the strangers. They watched impassively and used sign language to ask who the newcomers were, then returned to their tents to continue whatever it was they were doing before Coronado's army had appeared. The Spaniards, for their part, found the Querechos to be a curious folk. They were fascinated by these natives, and especially by their unique relationship with the buffalo. For these were buffalo Indians, and their existence and well-being on the plains were inextricably linked to the great herds.

"They followed the herd to provision themselves with meat," observed one Spaniard. "They neither grow nor harvest maize. With the [buffalo] skins they build their houses; with the skins they clothe and shoe themselves; from the skins they make rope and also obtain wool. With the sinews they make thread, with which they sew their clothes and also their tents. From the bones they shape awls. The dung they use for firewood, since there is no other fuel in that land. The bladders they use as jugs and drinking containers. They sustain themselves on the meat, eating it slightly roasted and heated over the dung. Some they eat raw."

Coronado interrogated the Querechos about Quivira. They professed ignorance of any such place, but they did speak of a great river—perhaps the Mississippi—to the east. The next day the Querechos packed up and went on their way. Coronado's party continued to drift in a vague south-easterly direction. They saw buffalo and more buffalo, occasional bands of Querechos passing in the distance, various wildlife, including prairie dogs, antelope, and gray wolves of an alarming size—but no sign of Quivira. The men were growing uneasy in this boundless, featureless sea of grass. The huge sky seemed to weigh down on them. Herds of buffalo rumbled past. At night the Spaniards gathered around their fires, unnerved by the vast darkness.

Was there no end to this strange place? Where was Quivira? Coronado sent Captain López and a small party on a reconnaissance to the east. After days of travel they returned with disappointing news: They had seen "nothing but cows and the sky." The conquistadores began casting dark glances at El Turco. The nervous Indian swore that Quivira was yet ahead. Coronado then asked the trusty Rodrigo Maldonado to ride ahead in search of the city. After four days of hard riding, Captain Maldonado came to a magnificent break in the plains, where the flatlands suddenly and dramatically gave way to a region of rough barrancas. Gazing out over these canyons, Maldonado and his men rejoiced. Here, finally, was land with detail and definition, an end to the great void of the plains. Along this striking escarpment there were many cool and surprisingly verdant canyons, formed by the headwaters of Texas rivers such as the Colorado, the Brazos, and the Red. There was good drinking water here, which drew not only an abundance of wildlife to the canyons but also a settlement of Native Americans.

It did not take long for Coronado and the main army to reach the barrancas. They entered one of the larger canyons—most likely Yellowhouse Canyon, not far from present-day Lubbock, Texas, although some historians believe that it was Palo Duro Canyon, near Amarillo—and made contact with the Indians in the late spring of 1541. These tattooed Indians were called "Teyas"—their name, according to some scholars, would eventually be given to the state of Texas. The Teyas Indians hunted buffalo as did the Querechos, but they also cultivated beans, raised turkeys, and gathered various fruits and nuts for food. They were not as nomadic as the Querechos but often dwelled

An Indian serves as interpreter for Coronado and a Wichita chief. The Spaniards finally reached Quivira—central Kansas—in July 1541. Once again, the conquistadores were gravely disappointed, for there was no gold in Quivira. Admitting defeat, Coronado called a halt to his quest and prepared to return to Mexico.

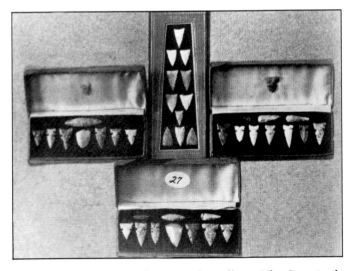

The Indians of Quivira had no gold, but they were master arrowhead makers, although these were of little interest to the Spaniards. Displayed here is a collection of exquisitely wrought arrowheads and lancets fashioned by Quiviran Indians.

in semipermanent *rancherías* in the valleys. The Spaniards gratefully settled down for a rest in the barranca. Their stay among the Teyas was uneventful except for the towering west Texas thunderstorm that blew up one day. The storm spawned a tornado—the Spaniards called it a "whirlwind"—and high winds and hail lashed the frightened explorers. Coronado was so thankful when the storm finally passed that he ordered the Franciscans to celebrate a thanksgiving mass. Thus, on May 23, 1541, 80 years before the Pilgrims gave thanks at Plymouth, the Spaniards gave thanks to God in Texas. They may well have dined on turkey afterward.

The Spaniards were not so grateful that they were ready to give up their wild and hopeless quest for gold, although some of them were becoming demoralized. The Teyas had no gold, and they also informed Coronado that Quivira was far to the north. The doomed El Turco continued to maintain that Quivira was just ahead, while Sopete insisted that his companion was lying. In late May 1541, Coronado called a meeting of his captains. After considerable debate, the council agreed that Coronado and 30 of his best men would ride north in a last-ditch attempt to find Quivira. The rest of the expedition, under the command of Captain Arellano, would return to Tiguex.

In early June, Coronado and his 30 men rode northward by the direction of a magnetized needle, accompanied by Teyas guides and Sopete. (El Turco was back in chains.) By the end of June they had entered present-day Kansas. They reached the Arkansas River and crossed it near the present-day town of Ford. Keeping to the north bank of the river, they followed it downstream. Soon they encountered native "Quivirans"—most likely Wichita Indians—out hunting buffalo. Farther downstream, the Spaniards finally encountered Quiviran settlements. But instead of the rich towns they expected, they found only rude villages of round, thatched-grass lodges. The Wichitas had no gold. Stubbornly, Coronado led his men deeper into Kansas. It was pleasant country—later settlers would find it to be some of the richest farmland in the United States—but there was no gold. By the end of July, even the ever-hopeful Coronado had finally recognized that further exploration was fruitless, and he called an end to this final reconnaissance.

Before they began the long journey homeward, the Spaniards decided to settle the issue of El Turco. Subjected to a fearful interrogation by his captors, the unfortunate Indian broke down and confessed. He admitted that he had been lying all along in an attempt to misguide the expedition. The people of Cicuye, angry at the rough treatment of Bigotes and Cacique, had convinced El Turco to lead the conquistadores out onto the high plains, hoping that they would become lost and perish. Coronado listened to this confession and then passed judgment on El Turco, who was quickly garroted and buried, after which the Spaniards set out for Tiguex. By September 1541, they had rejoined the rest of the expedition and had reoccupied the pueblo of Alcanfor.

The Spaniards settled in for another winter on the banks of the Rio Grande. They were a frustrated, travel-worn,

(continued on page 89)

Something Worthwhile

Coronado on the march.

The conquistadores and missionaries who roamed the Spanish Southwest seldom lingered to contemplate the strange beauty of the region. When Coronado informed Viceroy Mendoza by letter that he had "decided to send men throughout all the surrounding regions in order to find out if there is anything worth while; to suffer every hardship rather than abandon this enterprise," he hoped to redeem his expenditure of time, energy, and money with the discovery of objects of immediate material value—preferably gold or silver—rather than unparalleled natural wonders such as the Grand Canyon or sophisticated cultures such as those of the Pueblo and Plains Indians. Though not completely unappreciative, Coronado and his captains found the Grand Canyon more an obstacle than a miracle of the creation, and their admiration of the architectural achievements of the Zunis and the landscape carved by nature was tempered by their disappointment at not finding magnificent Cíbola and their haste to reach a fairer land watered by a "river, flowing through the plains, which was two leagues wide, with fish as large as horses," ruled by a lord who was served at table with gold and silver utensils. The American artists who visited the Southwest several centuries after Coronado's entrada—a painter, Cristobal de Quesada, actually accompanied the expedition, but his works have not survived—found its history, beauty, and native cultures more profitable for their own purposes.

Richard Kern's Robidoux Pass, White Mountains, New Mexico, 1848.
Kern visited the Southwest as a member of the American explorer John
Frémont's disastrous fourth expedition.

Thomas Moran's Lower Gorge of the Grand Canyon, Arizona.
Moran's paintings of the Grand Canyon were very popular with
American viewers in the 1870s and served a documentary as well
as an artistic purpose: More than 300 years after Coronado and
his captains visited the Southwest, it remained a terra incognita
for most Americans.

Indian Squaws Playing Ball on the Prairie,
*by Seth Eastman, a 19th-century American
artist. Juan Jaramillo, one of Coronado's
caballeros, pronounced the prairies of
Kansas the "best land" the expedition had
encountered. Coronado himself said of Kansas
that the "country itself is the best I have ever
seen for producing all the products of Spain."*

At the same time that Coronado and his men were roaming
the Southwest, another conquistador, Hernando de Soto,
was exploring much of the Southeast. In the process, de Soto
discovered the Mississippi River (as depicted here), which in all
likelihood was the wide river filled with giant fish that El Turco
had told Coronado about.

Frederic Remington's Ridden Down. *One way in which the coming of the Spanish transformed the native cultures of the West was through the introduction of the horse. Those tribes that were the first to obtain horses quickly became the most powerful.*

Displaced by the spread of white civilization, an Indian family moves on in search of new territory. Coronado's entrada was the inevitable first step in the process whereby what would become the American West was wrested from its native peoples.

(continued from page 80)
and tired lot now, and during the long, cold months ahead there was little to do in the way of glory. Instead, they harassed the outlying natives of Tiguex for food and winter clothing. Cold days of inactivity and the fiery tortures of body lice led to complaints, ill feelings, and dissension among the Spaniards. Some of them began to drift off toward home. The decline of Coronado had begun.

On December 27, 1541, in an attempt to relieve the winter tedium, Coronado and Maldonado, his best friend, had a horse race. Coronado was pulling ahead on his steed when his saddle girth suddenly broke, throwing him off to one side. As Maldonado's horse passed by, it kicked Coronado violently in the head. The injury was quite serious, and for a while it was feared the captain-general would die. He slowly recovered, but the accident permanently undermined his health. If he still harbored any thoughts of renewing his explorations in the spring, he abandoned them now, for he feared that he might die soon, and he wanted to return to his wife and his home.

In early April 1542 the disillusioned and disgruntled troop of conquistadores set out on the long trail back to the Spanish settlements in Mexico. The once grand and proud army of conquerors was much changed, worn down by the toil and hardship of the entrada. A dazed Coronado no longer rode at the head of the column but was instead carried on a cowhide litter slung between two plodding mules. He kept the men who were still loyal to him as personal guards; the rest seemed to blame him for the entrada's lack of success and for the most part subtly ignored the captain-general during the long trek back to Mexico. Hungry, tired and dirty, grumbling among themselves, harassed by Indians who shot poisoned arrows at them, and with not an ounce of gold among the entire company, the Spaniards straggled back to Culiacán. In this inglorious manner the explorations of Coronado the conquistador came to an end.

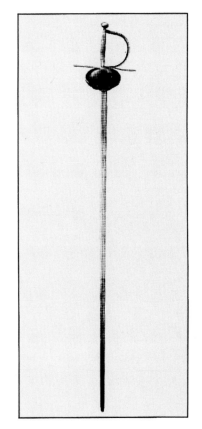

A conquistador's sword, on display at the National Museum in Mexico City. Many of the Native American tribes of the Southwest got a bitter taste of Spanish steel during the entrada of Coronado, and they were not sorry to see the Europeans go when they withdrew to Mexico in 1542.

Coronado's Legacy

At Culiacán, the expedition broke up. The company of adventurers who had spent almost two years together on the trail did not disband in an amicable manner. There was bitterness and pent-up animosity among them, and many old scores were settled in the courtyards of the town. Many of the conquistadores simply drifted off to whatever fate awaited them. Some, captivated by the vast spaces and harsh beauty of the Mexican landscape, stayed in Culiacán and lived out their remaining years on the edge of the frontier. One of those who did so was Pedro de Castañeda, whose account of the Coronado entrada, penned some 20 years later, is the most readable and reliable narrative of the expedition and remains an indispensable primary source. Those who still hungered for gold enlisted in other New World ventures. A few returned to Spain.

Tired of his administrative duties, in 1551 Viceroy Mendoza requested the king's permission to return to Spain. Instead, to Mendoza's horror, the king appointed him new viceroy of Peru. Mendoza went dutifully to South America and was dead within a year. (Incongruously, the gentle and moderate Mendoza was buried in Lima next to the savage Francisco Pizarro.) In the late 1540s, a crippled Fray Marcos de Niza, whose unfounded tales of the wonders of Cíbola were largely responsible for Coronado's entrada, retired to a monastery near the floating gardens of Xochimilco in Mexico City. He died in March 1558. The redoubtable Captain Cárdenas returned to Spain to claim

The Shrine of the Crucifix on the left side of the main altar of Santo Domingo Church in Mexico City. For centuries after his death, Coronado's bones lay rotting and all-but-forgotten beneath this shrine.

an inheritance; instead, he was subjected to years of incessant legal turmoil and long spells of imprisonment for his activities during the Cíbola entrada.

Captain Tovar fared better. He settled in Culiacán, married a lady of quality, and rose to the important post of *alcalde* (mayor) in the growing frontier town. As for the remarkable Cabeza de Vaca, he went on to South America, where his exploits won him the post of governor of Paraguay. But his sympathetic treatment of the Indians made him extremely unpopular among certain powerful political factions, who contrived to have him thrown into prison, where he languished until shortly before his death in 1551.

Before he could get on with his own life, Coronado had to return to Mexico City and report to Viceroy Mendoza. This was a prospect that the ailing captain-general no doubt dreaded, for he would not be returning to Mexico City as a conquering hero bearing gold, silver and jewels to present to the viceroy but rather as a somewhat dazed wanderer who had failed to impose himself on the New World in the manner of the "great" conquistadores such as Cortés and Pizarro. Mendoza, who had financed the greater part of the entrada and expected a return on his investment, would not be overly pleased to see Coronado, who had nothing of material value to show for his time in the wilderness. The captain-general lingered in Culiacán until the end of June 1542, gathering his strength, his wits, and his nerve, and then, accompanied by a small remnant of his army, he traveled slowly to Mexico City.

Mendoza greeted Coronado somewhat frostily at first, but the viceroy, who was known as a compassionate man and who had always been a friend of Coronado's as well as his superior, did not subject the ailing conquistador to any undue tribulations. It was obvious to Mendoza that his friend had done the best he could and had suffered for his efforts as well. Coronado returned to his family and reassumed his position as governor of New Galicia, moved

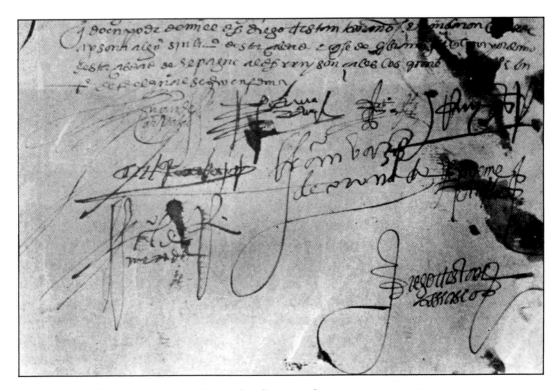

to the town of Guadalajara, and hoped to live out the rest of his years in peace. This was not to be, however, for there were men who did not share Mendoza's perspective on the issue of Coronado's entrada, and Coronado soon found himself embattled once again.

In the summer of 1544, word began to spread throughout Guadalajara and greater New Spain that Governor Coronado was to be subjected to a *residencia*—an inquisition—by representatives of the king of Spain. It was a grueling and often humiliating 50-day ordeal for the governor. His role as governor and as the leader of the entrada was scrutinized, and charges of mismanagement, corruption, and cruelty to the Indians were leveled. After all the evidence was gathered and all the witnesses heard, 12 of the charges were dismissed. But Coronado was found guilty on 13 other counts and was fined heavily and stripped of his governorship. And seven additional—and

In one of his final acts as a government functionary, Coronado affixed his signature to the official minutes of the Mexico City cabildo (governing council) in the summer of 1554. He died soon after.

more serious—charges were remanded to a higher court, the dreaded Council of the Indies. A pallid Coronado traveled to Mexico City, where his actions during the Cíbola entrada were subjected to further scrutiny. Fortunately, with the help of the influential Mendoza, Coronado was found innocent of all the remaining charges against him.

Coronado had survived the rigors of both the southwestern outback and the ponderous and often brutal imperial bureaucracy of Spain. But he had paid a price, for his physical and mental health were now in an irreversible decline. Nevertheless, he continued to play a role in the affairs of New Spain. He moved his family to Mexico City from Guadalajara and spent his days resting, entertaining visitors, and participating in city politics, twice serving on the *cabildo*, or governing council. But in the summer of 1554 he finally succumbed to the ill health that had plagued him since he had been kicked in the head by Maldonado's horse. On September 22, 1554, at the age of 44, Don Francisco Vázquez de Coronado passed away.

Coronado and his conquistadores had found no gold or

other riches in the Southwest, so there was little reason for any of them to return to the lands of the pueblo Indians or the wandering Querechos. But the Franciscan missionaries who took part in the entrada saw things in a different way. For them, the deserts and cordilleras and high plains of the southwestern interior represented a kind of spiritual El Dorado, a place where a great multitude of pagan souls were waiting to be brought into the fold of Christianity. While the bold horse soldiers of the Cíbola entrada drifted off to other lands or settled down in Mexico, the far less glamorous soldiers of God, who did not ride great steeds but rather sat astride plodding mules or simply walked, were attempting to establish a permanent presence in the Southwest.

One of the entrada friars to stay behind when Coronado pulled out of Cicuye was the elderly Fray Luis de Úbeda, who hoped his young black companion, Cristobal, would learn the language of the Indians, thereby enabling him to convert them to Christianity. Like many of the New World missionaries, the fate of Fray Luis remains unknown. The last white men to see him alive were members

After Coronado's entrada, armed Spanish incursions from Mexico into the Southwest ceased. But the Spanish missionaries—most of them were Franciscans—were not so easily discouraged, and they maintained a presence on the frontier despite the many dangers they faced.

The redoubtable Fray Juan de Padilla bestows a blessing on some Quiviran Indians. Although many of the Native Americans of the Southwest resisted Christianity, missionaries such as Padilla established a firm evangelical foothold, and Catholicism still flourishes there today.

of Coronado's force, and he was most likely killed not long after the conquistadores left the region. Despite the peaceful intentions of the priests, the behavior of the other Spaniards had not endeared them to the Indians, and the men of the cloth would often bear the brunt of the Native Americans' fear of and anger toward white people.

The intrepid Fray Juan de Padilla also chose to stay behind when the entrada ended. Receiving permission from the captain-general to return to Quivira, he journeyed to the Kansas plains, where he was well received by the Wichita Indians. But during a trip to visit a neighboring tribe, Fray Juan and several companions were attacked by Sioux warriors, who were angry because the

priest associated with their enemies. Fray Juan de Padilla was killed, thus becoming the first known Catholic martyr in the United States.

Three members of Fray Juan's entourage managed to escape the Indians' wrath, however. Two of them, Tarascan Indians named Lucas and Sebastian, had been made *donados*, or lay brothers, of the Catholic church. Following the murder of Fray Juan, these two wanderers embarked on a southwestern odyssey much like the one endured by Cabeza de Vaca and Esteban. Somehow, Lucas and Sebastian managed to find their way out of the wilderness and one day, years after the death of Fray Juan, they appeared at their old monastery in the region of Jalisco, on Mexico's west coast, with a remarkable story.

A third member of Fray Juan's party also survived. Andres de Campo, a Portuguese adventurer, was held captive by the Indians for 10 months before he escaped. Traveling with two dogs he had "liberated" from the Indians, the lucky man eventually found his way to the town of Tampico, on Mexico's east coast. His hair and beard were reported to be exceptionally long, and his safe return was thought to be a miracle, which indeed it was.

In the decades following Coronado's entrada, the Spanish government, unlike the tenacious missionaries, lost interest in the lands Coronado had explored. There was no gold or silver there, after all, and the Spanish were preoccupied with establishing their control over Mexico. But gradually their sphere of settlement grew and moved northward toward the American Southwest. In 1581, Spanish reconnaissance expeditions were active once again in New Mexico, Arizona, and Texas, and by 1598, an attempt at a permanent colonization of Coronado's interior Southwest was under way.

The wealthy Spaniard Juan de Oñate, whose grandfather had served under Coronado, played the role of Mendoza for this turn-of-the-century expedition. Under Oñate's leadership, a caravan of adventurous would-be colonists penetrated deep into New Mexico and established a precarious settlement near the pueblo towns of the Rio Grande. The little town was called San Juan de los Caballeros. Oñate was appointed governor of the province of New Mexico. The governor then embarked on a series of adventures in the Southwest. After eight years, he was recalled to Mexico and given the same reward Coronado and Cárdenas had been given for their service in the wilderness—he was put on trial for various offenses. Found guilty, Oñate was exiled. In the meantime, the tiny colony he had founded on the Rio Grande had managed to survive.

In 1610 a new governor, Pedro de Peralta, arrived to replace Oñate. Peralta soon relocated the colonists to a new site farther to the south. This settlement, originally called La Villa de Santa Fe, would gradually become the principal Spanish city in New Mexico. For the next 70 years, more colonists arrived and Santa Fe grew. Unfortunately, these settlers encroached on Indian lands and encroached on the Native Americans' freedom as well. The Indians were regularly mistreated by the Spanish newcomers. Some were enslaved and forced to do heavy labor, and those who refused to convert to Christianity were punished. As the years went by, Indian resentment grew, and Navajo, Apache, and other tribes launched raids on the settlements. In 1680 the Pueblo Indians, led by a Tiwa Indian shaman called Popé and aided by the Apaches, carried off a massive revolt against the Spanish in New Mexico. Hundreds of Spaniards were killed and the entire Spanish population was driven from the province. The Indians' success was short-lived, however, for in 1693 Don Diego de Vargas bloodily reconquered New Mexico.

Following the retaking of New Mexico, the Spanish learned that beyond the pueblo territories grew a new and more dire threat to their small colonies. Tribes of fierce, armed, painted, nomadic—and mounted—warriors were now the scourge of the settlements. Horses had always given Spanish troops a distinct advantage over their Indian enemies. But now the Plains Indians, as well as the Utes and the Navajos, had their own herds, the offspring of horses stolen from the Spaniards. And the Indians, who had once been terrified of horses, were now the equals, in terms of riding skills, of the best Spanish caballeros. A

Don Diego de Vargas, the scourge of New Mexico. In 1693, Vargas led a bloody campaign against the Pueblo and Apache tribes of the interior, who had driven the Spanish from their homelands in a massive insurrection. Vargas retook New Mexico, an event that signaled the beginning of the end of the great Native American pueblo cultures of the Southwest.

raiding culture had developed, and now swarms of ferocious Navajos and Apaches (beset themselves by the even more ferocious Comanches) terrorized the southwestern frontier.

The resistance of the mounted Indians slowed down Spanish colonization of the Southwest during the 18th century. Spanish missionaries, however, continued to venture where others feared to tread. It is not surprising, then, that the last great Spanish expedition into the southwestern interior was led by a Franciscan. During the

1770s, the Spanish authorities, seeking to link their pre-carious frontier outposts in California and New Mexico, had often discussed the need for someone to explore the unknown lands between them. In 1776, a Franciscan answered the call, and preparations for an expedition began in Santa Fe.

The priest who was to lead this final expedition was 25-year-old Fray Silvestre Vélez de Escalante. He would be accompanied by another Franciscan, Fray Francisco Atanasio Dominguez, a guide and interpreter named Andre

Plains Indians hunting buffalo. By the 18th century, tribes such as the Apaches and the Comanches were expert horse breeders and riders, and the Spaniards, who had introduced horses to the region back in Coronado's time, no longer enjoyed the advantage that had allowed them to dominate the Indians in military confrontations.

Muñiz, a cartographer named Bernardo de Miera, and other adventurers who brought the company's number to 10. On July 29, 1776, this group left the plaza of Santa Fe for an extended sojourn into the heart of the American West.

For five months the Escalante expedition traveled the rough lands beyond the headwaters of the San Juan Mountains. They scrambled along the western slopes of the Rocky Mountains and became the first white men to traverse the canyon lands of the upper Colorado River. They mapped many of that area's confusing rivers and made first contact with a dozen Native American tribes. Roaming through western Colorado, Utah's Great Basin, and the rugged lands around Arizona's Grand Canyon, they traced a great circle of discovery some 2,000 miles long. Fray Escalante kept a journal throughout the expedition, recording numerous geographic observations in detail.

The final objective of Escalante's journey was the Spanish settlement of Monterey in California. This goal was abandoned in October, however, when the expedition was still hundreds of miles to the east of Monterey. Winter was rapidly approaching, and the travelers wisely decided to swing southward back to Santa Fe before the worst snows came. Although the Escalante expedition failed to pioneer a route between Santa Fe and Monterey, it did provide a crucial link between the era of Spanish exploration in the Southwest and the subsequent explorations engaged in by Americans from the East. Bernardo de Miera prepared several versions of the map he had drawn during the expedition. This map, along with Escalante's diary, would be studied by generations of future explorers of the continental interior. The German explorer Baron Alexander von Humboldt, for example, relied on these materials in preparing his own influential map during an extended stay in Mexico. On his way back to Europe in 1804, Humboldt gave a copy of his map—which included much of Miera's work—to President Thomas Jefferson. Jefferson in turn

made this map known to the American explorer/spy Zebulon Pike, who, moving westward from St. Louis, engaged in the first tentative probings of the American Southwest sponsored by the U.S. government. Pike's appearance in Spanish territory on the Rio Grande in 1806 completed a transcontinental circle of discovery that had been started by Coronado more than two centuries before.

But by the time Zebulon Pike reached the banks of the Rio Grande, Don Francisco Vázquez de Coronado and his Cíbola entrada had been largely forgotten. Following his death, Coronado's name and his achievements as an explorer fell into obscurity. For three centuries, his role

A map of New Mexico drawn by the cartographer of the Escalante expedition, Bernardo de Miera, in 1776. Miera's map eventually found its way into the hands of U.S. president Thomas Jefferson, who passed it on to the explorer Zebulon Pike in 1806.

in the great age of Spanish exploration was seemingly ignored by history. Even Coronado's final resting place, in the old Church of Santo Domingo in Mexico City, was lost for many years. His achievements and his bones remained buried in a forsaken tomb until the mid-19th century, when interest in the American Southwest prompted new historical investigations into the significant part played by Coronado in the exploration of that previously unexplored territory. Upon disinterring the story of Coronado and his captains, modern historians learned that the accomplishments of the young conquistador were comparable to those of his more celebrated contemporaries. And today, the name Coronado is mentioned alongside names such as Cortés, Pizarro, and Balboa and graces numerous restaurants, hotels, motels, schools, highways, and streets

Lieutenant Zebulon Montgomery Pike. In 1806, Pike led an expedition from St. Louis across the Rocky Mountains to New Mexico's Rio Grande, setting in motion the process that would make these lands, once claimed for Spain by Coronado, a permanent part of the United States of America.

in the American Southwest. The captain-general would have been pleased.

And indeed, Coronado did much. In a span of less than 2 years, he covered 2,500 miles of the rough, dry, and frequently perilous American Southwest—a prodigious feat, even for the hardy Spanish conquistadores. For the first time, an organized European expedition penetrated deep into the mysterious interior of North America, and the information Coronado brought back provided the first evidence of the enormous size of the continent, while the detailed reconnaissance missions undertaken by Coronado's captains, who ranged through New Mexico, Arizona, California, Texas, and Kansas, gave Europeans the first truly accurate picture of the terrain of the Southwest—the mountains, rivers, forests, canyons, deserts, and prairies that awaited future explorers and settlers. Coronado's entrada also produced the first significant factual ethnological information concerning the Native Americans of the southwestern interior, including the Zunis, the Hopis, and the Opatas; the pueblo dwellers of the Rio Grande valley; the Querechos of the buffalo plains; the Teyas of the barrancas; and the Wichitas of Kansas.

But Coronado was not simply an ethnographer or geographer, for he himself occupies a place in the history of North America and its peoples. When that history is discussed, it is the English settlers, the Pilgrims who colonized the Atlantic Coast, who are cited as the "first" white Americans. But long before the Pilgrims landed at Plymouth, Spaniards were riding across lands that are today considered to be the very heartland of America, for the part of Kansas that Coronado reached before he abandoned his quest for Quivira lies at the geographical center of the United States. Explorers, adventurers, missionaries, mountain men, seekers of fur and silver and gold, and settlers of all kinds would eventually come to the American Southwest—but Coronado and his captains were there first.

A recently discovered burial site of Quiviran Indians in Kansas. The Quivirans, according to Coronado, were friendly, handsome, and physically impressive; most of the men measured more than "10 palms" (7 feet) tall. Along with many other Native American peoples, the Quivirans did not survive the coming of the Europeans that began with the entrada of Coronado.

Further Reading

Anderson, Joan. *Spanish Pioneers of the Southwest*. New York: Lodestar Books, 1988.

Bakeless, John. *America As Seen by Its First Explorers*. New York: Dover, 1961.

Bernal-Diaz, Del Castillo. *Conquest of New Spain*. New York: Penguin Books, 1963.

Bolton, Herbert E. *Coronado, Knight of Pueblos and Plains*. New York: Whittlesey House, 1949.

Collis, Maurice. *Cortez and Montezuma*. New York: Avon Books, 1978.

Day, Arthur G. *Coronado's Quest: The Discovery of the Southwestern States*. Westport, CT: Greenwood Press, 1982.

Dobie, Frank J. *Coronado's Children: Tales of Lost and Buried Treasures of the Southwest*. Darby, PA: Darby Books, 1982.

Dominguez, Jorge I. *Insurrection of Loyalty: The Breakdown of the Spanish-American Empire*. Cambridge: Harvard University Press, 1980.

Everett, Dianna, ed. *Coronado and the Myth of Quivira*. Canyon, TX: Panhandle–Plains Historical Society, 1985.

Forbes, Jack D. *Apache, Navaho, and Spaniard*. Westport, CT: Greenwood Press, 1980.

Gibson, Charles. *Spain in America*. New York: HarperCollins, 1968.

Haring, Clarence H. *The Spanish Empire in America*. New York: Harcourt Brace Jovanovich, 1963.

Hodge, F. W., and T. H. Lewis. *Spanish Explorers in the Southern United States 1528–1543*. Austin: Texas State Historical Association, 1984.

Johnson, William W. *Cortes: Conquering the New World*. New York: Paragon House, 1987.

———. *The Spanish West*. Needham Heights, MA: Silver Burdett, 1976.

Maynard, Theodore. *De Soto and the Conquistadores*. New York: AMS Press, 1930.

Sauer, Carl. *The Road to Cibola*. Berkeley: University of California Press, 1932.

Spicer, Edward H. *Cycles of Conquest: The Impact of Spain, Mexico, and the U.S. on Indians of the Southwest 1533–1960*. Tucson: University of Arizona Press, 1962.

Udall, Stewart L. *To the Inland Empire: Coronado and our Spanish Legacy*. Garden City, NY: Doubleday, 1987.

Wagner, Henry R. *The Spanish Southwest 1542–1794*. Salem, NH: Ayer, 1968.

Weber, David J., ed. *New Spain's Far Northern Frontier: Essays on Spain in the American West*. Dallas: Southern Methodist University Press, 1988.

Wepman, Dennis. *Cortés*. New York: Chelsea House, 1986.

Whitman, Sylvia. *Hernando de Soto and the Explorers of the American South*. New York: Chelsea House, 1991.

Chronology

Entries in roman refer directly to Francisco Vásquez de Coronado and the exploration of the Southwest; entries in italic refer to important historical and cultural events of the era.

1492   *Christopher Columbus, trying to find a western sea route to China, lands on the island of Hispaniola, becoming the first European to reach the New World*

1497   *Vasco da Gama, sailing for Portugal, rounds the Cape of Good Hope, opening a sea route to the Indies*

Early 1500s   *Spanish caravels first appear on the Atlantic coasts of the Americas; the entradas—inland expeditions in search of gold and wealth—commence; the age of the conquistador begins*

1518   Hernán Cortés conquers the Aztec empire and dispatches expeditions throughout Mexico and Central America; *Portuguese navigator Ferdinand Magellan embarks on his journey to circumnavigate the globe*

1528   Esteban de Dorantes (Stephen the Moor, a former slave) and Álvar Núñez Cabeza de Vaca are the first non-Indians to explore what is today the southwestern United States

1532   *Francisco Pizarro conquers the Incas and plunders Peru*

1535   Francisco Vásquez de Coronado comes to Mexico to seek his fortune

1536   Esteban and Cabeza de Vaca tell Don Antonio de Mendoza, viceroy of New Spain, about lands of great riches to the north

1538   Coronado appointed governor of New Galicia

1539   Esteban and Fray Marcos de Niza explore Northern Mexico; Zuni Indians kill Esteban and several of his followers; Niza returns to Culiacán and reports to Coronado rumors of wealthy cities to the north; Mendoza appoints Coronado captain-general of the Cíbola expedition

1540	Coronado and 337 troops set forth in search of Cíbola; Coronado's cavalry defeats the Zuni at Hawikuh; members of Coronado's party become the first Europeans to see the Grand Canyon and to enter present-day California; Coronado settles his men in the region of Tiguex
1541	*De Soto discovers the Mississppi River;* urged eastward by Indian stories of the wealthy kingdom of Quivira, Coronado crosses the Pecos River and the Llano Estacado; reaches present-day Kansas in June; ends eastern reconaissance and returns to Tiguex; suffers a head injury in a horse race in December
1542	Coronado and his men return to Culiacán
1544	Coronado charged with numerous counts of mismanagement, corruption, and cruelty to Indians; cleared of all but minor charges
1554	Coronado dies in September
1581	Building on the missionary work of the preceding decades, Spanish expeditions spread out across what is now New Mexico, Arizona, and Texas
1610	Pedro de Peralta, a Spanish governor, establishes La Villa de Santa Fe, the principal Spanish city in New Mexico
1680	Pueblo Indians, led by Popé, revolt against the Spanish and temporarily drive them from New Mexico
1693	Don Diego de Vargas takes back New Mexico from the Indians
July 1776	The Spanish dispatch expeditions to establish a link between posts in California and New Mexico; Bernardo de Miera makes maps of the route and of the surrounding terrain

Index

Picture Credits

John Miller Morris is a geography professor, environmental historian, and urban planner. He grew up on the Navajo reservation of Arizona and New Mexico and the high plains of West Texas. From an early age, he delighted in the picturesque Coronado country and imbibed the legends and lore of the famous expedition. With his daughter, Claire, he has attempted to retrace Coronado's route from the Rio Grande across the Llano Estacado to the mysterious barranca of the eastern escarpment.

William H. Goetzmann holds the Jack S. Blanton, Sr., Chair in History at the University of Texas at Austin, where he has taught for many years. The author of numerous works on American history and exploration, he won the 1967 Pulitzer and Parkman prizes for his *Exploration and Empire: The Role of the Explorer and Scientist in the Winning of the American West, 1800–1900*. With his son William N. Goetzmann, he coauthored *The West of the Imagination*, which received the Carr P. Collins Award in 1986 from the Texas Institute of Letters. His documentary television series of the same name received a blue ribbon in the history category at the American Film and Video Festival held in New York City in 1987. A recent work, *New Lands, New Men: America and the Second Great Age of Discovery*, was published in 1986 to much critical acclaim.

Michael Collins served as command module pilot on the *Apollo 11* space mission, which landed his colleagues Neil Armstrong and Buzz Aldrin on the moon. A graduate of the United States Military Academy, Collins was named an astronaut in 1963. In 1966 he piloted the *Gemini 10* mission, during which he became the third American to walk in space. The author of several books on space exploration, Collins was director of the Smithsonian Institution's National Air and Space Museum from 1971 to 1978 and is a recipient of the Presidential Medal of Freedom.